FAHRENHEIT 451

Ray Bradbury

SPARK PUBLISHING

SPARKNOTES is a registered trademark of SparkNotes LLC

Spark Publishing
A Division of Barnes & Noble
120 Fifth Avenue
New York, NY 10011
www.sparknotes.com

ISBN-13: 978-1-4114-0512-7
ISBN-10: 1-4114-0512-9

Please submit changes or report errors to www.sparknotes.com/errors.

Printed in the United States.

10 9 8 7 6 5 4 3 2

CONTENTS

CONTEXT

Ray bradbury was born in Waukegan, Illinois, on August 22, 1920. By the time he was eleven, he had already begun writing his own stories on butcher paper. His family moved fairly frequently, and he graduated from a Los Angeles high school in 1938. He had no further formal education, but he studied on his own at the library and continued to write. For several years, he earned money by selling newspapers on street corners. His first published story was "Hollerbochen's Dilemma," which appeared in 1938 in *Imagination!*, a magazine for amateur writers. In 1942 he was published in *Weird Tales*, the legendary pulp science-fiction magazine that fostered such luminaries of the genre as H. P. Lovecraft. Bradbury honed his sci-fi sensibility writing for popular television shows, including *Alfred Hitchcock Presents* and *The Twilight Zone*. He also ventured into screenplay writing (he wrote the screenplay for John Huston's 1953 film *Moby Dick*). His book *The Martian Chronicles*, published in 1950, established his reputation as a leading American writer of science fiction.

In the spring of 1950, while living with his family in a humble home in Venice, California, Bradbury began writing what was to become *Fahrenheit 451* on pay-by-the-hour typewriters in the University of California at Los Angeles library basement. He finished the first draft, a shorter version called *The Fireman*, in just nine days. Following in the futuristic-dustpan tradition of George Orwell's *1984*, *Fahrenheit 451* was published in 1953 and became Bradbury's most popular and widely read work of fiction. He produced a stage version of the novel at the Studio Theatre Playhouse in Los Angeles. The seminal French New Wave director François Truffaut also made a critically acclaimed film adaptation in 1967.

Bradbury has received many awards for his writing and has been honored in numerous ways. Most notably, Apollo astronauts named the Dandelion Crater on the moon after his novel *Dandelion Wine*. In addition to his novels, screenplays, and scripts for television, Bradbury has written two musicals, co-written two "space-age cantatas," collaborated on an Academy Award–nominated animation short called *Icarus Montgolfier Wright*, and started his own television series, *The Ray Bradbury Theatre*. Bradbury, who still lives in California, continues to write and is acknowledged as one of the masters of the science-fiction genre. Although he is recognized primarily for his ideas and sometimes denigrated for his writing style (which some find alternately dry and maudlin), Bradbury nonetheless retains his place among important literary science-fiction talents and visionaries like Jules Verne, H. P. Lovecraft, George Orwell, Arthur C. Clarke, and Philip K. Dick.

PLOT OVERVIEW

Guy Montag is a fireman who burns books in a futuristic American city. In Montag's world, firemen start fires rather than putting them out. The people in this society do not read books, enjoy nature, spend time by themselves, think independently, or have meaningful conversations. Instead, they drive very fast, watch excessive amounts of television on wall-size sets, and listen to the radio on "Seashell Radio" sets attached to their ears.

Montag encounters a gentle seventeen-year-old girl named Clarisse McClellan, who opens his eyes to the emptiness of his life with her innocently penetrating questions and her unusual love of people and nature. Over the next few days, Montag experiences a series of disturbing events. First, his wife, Mildred, attempts suicide by swallowing a bottle of sleeping pills. Then, when he responds to an alarm that an old woman has a stash of hidden literature, the woman shocks him by choosing to be burned alive along with her books. A few days later, he hears that Clarisse has been killed by a speeding car. Montag's dissatisfaction with his life increases, and he begins to search for a solution in a stash of books that he has stolen from his own fires and hidden inside an air-conditioning vent.

When Montag fails to show up for work, his fire chief, Beatty, pays a visit to his house. Beatty explains that it's normal for a fireman to go through a phase of wondering what books have to offer, and he delivers a dizzying monologue explaining how books came to be banned in the first place. According to Beatty, special-interest groups and other "minorities" objected to books that offended them. Soon, books all began to look the same, as writers tried to avoid offending anybody. This was not enough, however, and society as a whole decided to simply burn books rather than permit conflicting opinions. Beatty tells Montag to take twenty-four hours or so to see if his stolen books contain anything worthwhile and then turn them in for incineration. Montag begins a long and frenzied night of reading.

Overwhelmed by the task of reading, Montag looks to his wife for help and support, but she prefers television to her husband's company and cannot understand why he would want to take the terrible risk of reading books. He remembers that he once met a retired English professor named Faber sitting in a park, and he decides that this man might be able to help him understand what he reads. He visits Faber, who tells him that the value of books lies in the detailed awareness of life that they contain. Faber says that Montag needs not only books but also the leisure to read them and the freedom to act upon their ideas.

Faber agrees to help Montag with his reading, and they concoct a risky scheme to overthrow the status quo. Faber will contact a printer and begin reproducing books, and Montag will plant books in the homes of firemen to discredit the profession and to destroy the machinery of censorship. Faber gives him a two-way radio earpiece (the "green bullet") so that he can hear what Montag hears and talk to him secretly.

Montag goes home, and soon two of his wife's friends arrive to watch television. The women discuss their families and the war that is about to be declared in an extremely frivolous manner. Their superficiality angers him, and he takes out a book of poetry and reads "Dover Beach" by Matthew Arnold. Faber buzzes in his ear for him to be quiet, and Mildred tries to explain that the poetry reading is a standard way for firemen to demonstrate the uselessness of literature. The women are extremely disturbed by the poem and leave to file a complaint against Montag.

Montag goes to the fire station and hands over one of his books to Beatty. Beatty confuses Montag by barraging him with contradictory quotations from great books. Beatty exploits these contradictions to show that literature is morbid and dangerously complex, and that it deserves incineration. Suddenly, the alarm sounds, and they rush off to answer the call, only to find that the alarm is at Montag's own house. Mildred gets into a cab with her suitcase, and Montag realizes that his own wife has betrayed him.

Beatty forces Montag to burn the house himself; when he is done, Beatty places him under arrest. When Beatty continues to berate Montag, Montag turns the flamethrower on his superior and proceeds to burn him to ashes. Montag knocks the other firemen unconscious and runs. The Mechanical Hound, a monstrous machine that Beatty has set to attack Montag, pounces and injects Montag's leg with a large dose of anesthetic. Montag manages to destroy it with his flamethrower; then he walks off the numbness in his leg and escapes with some books that were hidden in his backyard. He hides these in another fireman's house and calls in an alarm from a pay phone.

Montag goes to Faber's house, where he learns that a new Hound has been put on his trail, along with several helicopters and a television crew. Faber tells Montag that he is leaving for St. Louis to see a retired printer who may be able to help them. Montag gives Faber some money and tells him how to remove Montag's scent from his house so the Hound will not enter it. Montag then takes some of Faber's old clothes and runs off toward the river. The whole city watches as the chase unfolds on TV, but Montag manages to escape in the river and change into Faber's clothes to disguise his scent. He drifts downstream into the country and follows a set of abandoned railroad tracks until he finds a group of renegade intellectuals ("the Book People"), led by a man named Granger, who welcome him. They are a part of a nationwide network of book lovers who have memorized many great works of literature and philosophy. They hope that they may be of some help to mankind in the aftermath of the war that has just been declared. Montag's role is to memorize the Book of Ecclesiastes. Enemy jets appear in the sky and completely obliterate the city with bombs. Montag and his new friends move on to search for survivors and rebuild civilization.

Character List

Guy Montag A third-generation fireman who suddenly realizes the emptiness of his life and starts to search for meaning in the books he is supposed to be burning. Though he is sometimes rash and has a hard time thinking for himself, he is determined to break free from the oppression of ignorance. He quickly forms unusually strong attachments with anyone who seems receptive to true friendship. His biggest regret in life is not having a better relationship with his wife.

Mildred Montag Montag's brittle, sickly looking wife. She is obsessed with watching television and refuses to engage in frank conversation with her husband about their marriage or her feelings. Her suicide attempt, which she refuses even to acknowledge, clearly indicates that she harbors a great deal of pain. Small-minded and childish, Mildred does not understand her husband and apparently has no desire to do so.

Captain Beatty The captain of Montag's fire department. Although he is himself extremely well-read, paradoxically he hates books and people who insist on reading them. He is cunning and devious, and so perceptive that he appears to read Montag's thoughts.

Professor Faber A retired English professor whom Montag encountered a year before the book opens. Faber still possesses a few precious books and aches to have more. He readily admits that the current state of society is due to the cowardice of people like himself, who would not speak out against book burning when they still could have stopped it. He berates himself for being a coward, but he shows himself capable of acts that require great courage and place him in considerable danger.

Clarisse McClellan   A beautiful seventeen-year-old who introduces Montag to the world's potential for beauty and meaning with her gentle innocence and curiosity. She is an outcast from society because of her odd habits, which include hiking, playing with flowers, and asking questions, but she and her (equally odd) family seem genuinely happy with themselves and each other.

Granger   The leader of the "Book People," the group of hobo intellectuals Montag finds in the country. Granger is intelligent, patient, and confident in the strength of the human spirit. He is committed to preserving literature through the current Dark Age.

Mrs. Phelps   One of Mildred's vapid friends. She is emotionally disconnected from her life, appearing unconcerned when her third husband is sent off to war. Yet she breaks down crying when Montag reads her a poem, revealing suppressed feelings and sensibilities.

Mrs. Bowles   One of Mildred's friends. Like Mrs. Phelps, she does not seem to care deeply about her own miserable life, which includes one divorce, one husband killed in an accident, one husband who commits suicide, and two children who hate her. Both of Mildred's friends are represented as typical specimens of their society.

Stoneman and Black   Two firemen who work with Montag. They share the lean, shadowed look common to all firemen and go about their jobs unquestioningly.

ANALYSIS OF MAJOR CHARACTERS

GUY MONTAG

Appropriately named after a paper-manufacturing company, Montag is the protagonist of *Fahrenheit 451*. He is by no means a perfect hero, however. The reader can sympathize with Montag's mission, but the steps he takes toward his goal often seem clumsy and misguided. Montag's faith in his profession and his society begins to decline almost immediately after the novel's opening passage. Faced with the enormity and complexity of books for the first time, he is often confused, frustrated, and overwhelmed. As a result, he has difficulty deciding what to do independently of Beatty, Mildred, or Faber. Likewise, he is often rash, inarticulate, self-obsessed, and too easily swayed. At times he is not even aware of why he does things, feeling that his hands are acting by themselves. These subconscious actions can be quite horrific, such as when he finds himself setting his supervisor on fire, but they also represent his deepest desires to rebel against the status quo and find a meaningful way to live.

In his desperate quest to define and comprehend his own life and purpose by means of books, he blunders blindly and stupidly as often as he thinks and acts lucidly. His attempts to reclaim his own humanity range from the compassionate and sensitive, as in his conversations with Clarisse, to the grotesque and irresponsible, as in his murder of Beatty and his half-baked scheme to overthrow the firemen.

MILDRED MONTAG

Mildred is the one major character in the book who seems to have no hope of resolving the conflicts within herself. Her suicide attempt suggests that she is in great pain and that her obsession with television is a means to avoid confronting her life. But her true feelings are buried very deep within her. She even appears to be unaware of her own suicide attempt. She is a frightening character, because the reader would expect to know the protagonist's wife very intimately, but she is completely cold, distant, and unreadable. Her betrayal of

Montag is far more severe than Beatty's, since she is, after all, his wife. Bradbury portrays Mildred as a shell of a human being, devoid of any sincere emotional, intellectual, or spiritual substance. Her only attachment is to the "family" in the soap opera she watches.

CAPTAIN BEATTY

Beatty is a complex character, full of contradictions. He is a book burner with a vast knowledge of literature, someone who obviously cared passionately about books at some point. It is important to note that Beatty's entire speech to Montag describing the history of the firemen is strangely ambivalent, containing tones of irony, sarcasm, passion, and regret, all at once. Beatty calls books treacherous weapons, yet he uses his own book learning to manipulate Montag mercilessly.

In one of his most sympathetic moments, Beatty says he's tried to understand the universe and knows firsthand its melancholy tendency to make people feel bestial and lonely. He is quick to stress that he prefers his life of instant pleasure, but it is easy to get the impression that his vehemence serves to deny his true feelings. His role as a character is complicated by the fact that Bradbury uses him to do so much explication of the novel's background. In his shrewd observations of the world around him and his lack of any attempt to prevent his own death, he becomes too sympathetic to function as a pure villain.

PROFESSOR FABER

Named after a famous publisher, Faber competes with Beatty in the struggle for Montag's mind. His control over Montag may not be as complete and menacing as Beatty's, but he does manipulate Montag via his two-way radio to accomplish the things his cowardice has prevented him from doing himself, acting as the brain directing Montag's body. Faber's role and motivations are complex: at times he tries to help Montag think independently and at other times he tries to dominate him. Similarly, he can be cowardly and heroic by turns. Neither Faber nor Beatty can articulate his beliefs in a completely convincing way, despite the fact that their pupil is naïve and credulous.

THEMES, MOTIFS & SYMBOLS

THEMES

Themes are the fundamental and often universal ideas explored in a literary work.

CENSORSHIP

Fahrenheit 451 doesn't provide a single, clear explanation of why books are banned in the future. Instead, it suggests that many different factors could combine to create this result. These factors can be broken into two groups: factors that lead to a general lack of interest in reading and factors that make people actively hostile toward books. The novel doesn't clearly distinguish these two developments. Apparently, they simply support one another.

The first group of factors includes the popularity of competing forms of entertainment such as television and radio. More broadly, Bradbury thinks that the presence of fast cars, loud music, and advertisements creates a lifestyle with too much stimulation in which no one has the time to concentrate. Also, the huge mass of published material is too overwhelming to think about, leading to a society that reads condensed books (which were very popular at the time Bradbury was writing) rather than the real thing.

The second group of factors, those that make people hostile toward books, involves envy. People don't like to feel inferior to those who have read more than they have. But the novel implies that the most important factor leading to censorship is the objections of special-interest groups and "minorities" to things in books that offend them. Bradbury is careful to refrain from referring specifically to racial minorities—Beatty mentions dog lovers and cat lovers, for instance. The reader can only try to infer which special-interest groups he really has in mind.

As the Afterword to *Fahrenheit 451* demonstrates, Bradbury is extremely sensitive to any attempts to restrict his free speech; for instance, he objects strongly to letters he has received suggesting that he revise his treatment of female or black characters. He sees such interventions as essentially hostile and intolerant—as the first step on the road to book burning.

KNOWLEDGE VERSUS IGNORANCE

Montag, Faber, and Beatty's struggle revolves around the tension between knowledge and ignorance. The fireman's duty is to destroy knowledge and promote ignorance in order to equalize the population and promote sameness. Montag's encounters with Clarisse, the old woman, and Faber ignite in him the spark of doubt about this approach. His resultant search for knowledge destroys the unquestioning ignorance he used to share with nearly everyone else, and he battles the basic beliefs of his society.

MOTIFS

Motifs are recurring structures, contrasts, and literary devices that can help to develop and inform the text's major themes.

PARADOXES

In the beginning of "The Hearth and the Salamander," Montag's bedroom is described first as "not empty" and then as "indeed empty," because Mildred is physically there, but her thoughts and feelings are elsewhere. Bradbury's repeated use of such paradoxical statements—especially that a character or thing is dead *and* alive or there *and* not there—is frequently applied to Mildred, suggesting her empty, half-alive condition. Bradbury also uses these paradoxical statements to describe the "Electric-Eyed Snake" stomach pump and, later, the Mechanical Hound. These paradoxes question the reality of beings that are apparently living but spiritually dead. Ultimately, Mildred and the rest of her society seem to be not much more than machines, thinking only what they are told to think. The culture of *Fahrenheit 451* is a culture of insubstantiality and unreality, and Montag desperately seeks more substantial truths in the books he hoards.

ANIMAL AND NATURE IMAGERY

Animal and nature imagery pervades the novel. Nature is presented as a force of innocence and truth, beginning with Clarisse's adolescent, reverent love for nature. She convinces Montag to taste the rain, and the experience changes him irrevocably. His escape from the city into the country is a revelation to him, showing him the enlightening power of unspoiled nature.

Much of the novel's animal imagery is ironic. Although this society is obsessed with technology and ignores nature, many frightening mechanical devices are modeled after or named for animals, such as the Electric-Eyed Snake machine and the Mechanical Hound.

RELIGION

Fahrenheit 451 contains a number of religious references. Mildred's friends remind Montag of icons he once saw in a church and did not understand. The language Bradbury uses to describe the enameled, painted features of the artifacts Montag saw is similar to the language he uses to describe the firemen's permanent smiles. Faber invokes the Christian value of forgiveness: after Montag turns against society, Faber reminds him that since he was once one of the faithful, he should demonstrate pity rather than fury.

The narrative also contains references to the miracle at Canaa, where Christ transformed water into wine. Faber describes himself as water and Montag as fire, asserting that the merging of the two will produce wine. In the biblical story, Jesus Christ's transformation of water into wine was one of the miracles that proved his identity and instilled faith in his role as the savior. Montag longs to confirm his own identity through a similar self-transformation.

The references to fire are more complex. In the Christian tradition, fire has several meanings: from the pagan blaze in which the golden calf was made to Moses' burning bush, it symbolizes both blatant heresy and divine presence. Fire in *Fahrenheit 451* also possesses contradictory meanings. At the beginning it is the vehicle of a restrictive society, but Montag turns it upon his oppressor, using it to burn Beatty and win his freedom.

Finally, Bradbury uses language and imagery from the Bible to resolve the novel. In the last pages, as Montag and Granger's group walk upriver to find survivors after the bombing of the city, Montag knows they will eventually talk, and he tries to remember appropriate passages from the Bible. He brings to mind Ecclesiastes 3:1, "To everything there is a season," and also Revelations 22:2, "And on either side of the river was there a tree of life . . . and the leaves of the tree were for the healing of the nations," which he decides to save for when they reach the city. The verse from Revelations also speaks of the holy city of God, and the last line of the book, "When we reach the city," implies a strong symbolic connection between the atomic holocaust of Montag's world and the Apocalypse of the Bible.

MOTIFS

SYMBOLS

Symbols are objects, characters, figures, and colors used to represent abstract ideas or concepts.

BLOOD

Blood appears throughout the novel as a symbol of a human being's repressed soul or primal, instinctive self. Montag often "feels" his most revolutionary thoughts welling and circulating in his blood. Mildred, whose primal self has been irretrievably lost, remains unchanged when her poisoned blood is replaced with fresh, mechanically administered blood by the Electric-Eyed Snake machine. The symbol of blood is intimately related to the Snake machine. Bradbury uses the electronic device to reveal Mildred's corrupted insides and the thick sediment of delusion, misery, and self-hatred within her. The Snake has explored "the layer upon layer of night and stone and stagnant spring water," but its replacement of her blood could not rejuvenate her soul. Her poisoned, replaceable blood signifies the empty lifelessness of Mildred and the countless others like her.

"THE HEARTH AND THE SALAMANDER"

Bradbury uses this conjunction of images as the title of the first part of *Fahrenheit 451*. The hearth, or fireplace, is a traditional symbol of the home; the salamander is one of the official symbols of the firemen, as well as the name they give to their fire trucks. Both of these symbols have to do with fire, the dominant image of Montag's life—the hearth because it contains the fire that heats a home, and the salamander because of ancient beliefs that it lives in fire and is unaffected by flames.

"THE SIEVE AND THE SAND"

The title of the second part of *Fahrenheit 451*, "The Sieve and the Sand," is taken from Montag's childhood memory of trying to fill a sieve with sand on the beach to get a dime from a mischievous cousin and crying at the futility of the task. He compares this memory to his attempt to read the whole Bible as quickly as possible on the subway in the hope that, if he reads fast enough, some of the material will stay in his memory.

Simply put, the sand is a symbol of the tangible truth Montag seeks, and the sieve the human mind seeking a truth that remains elusive and, the metaphor suggests, impossible to grasp in any permanent way.

THE PHOENIX

After the bombing of the city, Granger compares mankind to a phoenix that burns itself up and then rises out of its ashes over and over again. Man's advantage is his ability to recognize when he has made a mistake, so that eventually he will learn not to make that mistake anymore. Remembering the mistakes of the past is the task Granger and his group have set for themselves. They believe that individuals are not as important as the collective mass of culture and history. The symbol of the phoenix's rebirth refers not only to the cyclical nature of history and the collective rebirth of humankind but also to Montag's spiritual resurrection.

MIRRORS

At the very end of the novel, Granger says they must build a mirror factory to take a long look at themselves; this remark recalls Montag's description of Clarisse as a mirror in "The Hearth and the Salamander." Mirrors here are symbols of self-understanding, of seeing oneself clearly.

Summary & Analysis

The Hearth and the Salamander

From the opening through Montag's arrival at home

Summary

Guy Montag is a fireman in charge of burning books in a grim, futuristic United States. The book opens with a brief description of the pleasure he experiences while on the job one evening. He wears a helmet emblazoned with the numeral 451 (the temperature at which paper burns), a black uniform with a salamander on the arm, and a "phoenix disc" on his chest. On his way home from the fire station, he feels a sense of nervous anticipation. After suspecting a lingering nearby presence, he meets his new neighbor, an inquisitive and unusual seventeen-year-old named Clarisse McClellan. She immediately recognizes him as a fireman and seems fascinated by him and his uniform. She explains that she is "crazy" and proceeds to suggest that the original duty of firemen was to extinguish fires rather than to light them. She asks him about his job and tells him that she comes from a strange family that does such peculiar things as talk to each other and walk places (being a pedestrian, like reading, is against the law).

Clarisse's strangeness makes Guy nervous, and he laughs repeatedly and involuntarily. She reminds him in different ways of candlelight, a clock, and a mirror. He cannot help feeling somehow attracted to her: she fascinates him with her outrageous questions, unorthodox lifestyle, perceptive observations, and "incredible power of identification." She asks him if he is happy and then disappears into her house. Pondering the absurd question, he enters his house and muses about this enigmatic stranger and her comprehension of his "innermost trembling thought."

Analysis

"The Hearth and the Salamander" focuses on Montag's job as a fireman and his home life. The hearth, or fireplace, is a traditional symbol of the home, and the salamander is one of the official symbols of the firemen, as well as what they call their fire trucks. Both of these symbols have to do with fire, the dominant image of Montag's life—the hearth because it contains the fire that heats a home, and the salamander because of ancient beliefs that it lives in fire and is unaffected by flames. Montag enjoys his job burning books and takes great pride in it; at the beginning of the novel, it largely defines his character. The opening passage describes the pleasure he experiences while burning books. He loves the spectacle of burning and seeing things "changed" by the fire, and his fire-induced grin seldom leaves his face. He even loves the smell of kerosene, which never quite washes off his body, and which he describes to Clarisse as "perfume."

As we later learn, Montag's society has abandoned books in favor of hollow, frenetic entertainment and instant gratification. At the beginning of the novel, Montag, like everyone else, disdains what he does not understand, and by burning books he creates a spectacle that pleases the frightened masses. He has a position of respect in his society, and Clarisse's lack of respect or fear of his authority is one of the ways in which she first distinguishes herself from the general population.

Clarisse is extremely inquisitive and thoughtful, and she irritates Montag at first because she challenges his most deeply ingrained beliefs with her innocent questioning. In a society where reading, driving slowly, and walking outside for any length of time are outlawed and a candid conversation is a rare and suspicious event, Clarisse's gentle love of nature and people is truly peculiar. She is forced to go to a psychiatrist for strange behaviors such as hiking, catching butterflies, and thinking independently. Her family is responsible for teaching her to be so quietly rebellious, especially her uncle. At night, the McClellan house is lit up brightly, contrasting sharply with the darkness and silence of the other houses. Montag is ignorant of the past of which Clarisse speaks and accuses her of thinking too much. Nevertheless, Clarisse opens Montag's eyes to the beauties of the natural world, and she recognizes that he is not like everyone else and has the potential to be a thinking individual like her. Before their meeting, Montag's familiarity with nature was limited to his fascination with fire.

Montag's feelings toward Clarisse are ambivalent, a combination of fascination and repulsion. Clarisse removes Montag's mask of happiness, forcing him to confront the deeper reality of his situation, and his discomfort manifests itself in his involuntary bursts of spiteful, confused laughter. She seems like a mirror to him with her "incredible power of identification." He feels that she is profoundly connected to him somehow, as if she had been waiting for him. Later, looking back on his first encounter with her, Clarisse's face seems to presage further darkness before a new light.

THE HEARTH AND THE SALAMANDER (CONTINUED)

From Montag in his bedroom through the rain scene with Clarisse

SUMMARY

Montag is disturbed by his meeting with Clarisse because he is not used to talking with people about personal subjects. Upon returning home, he realizes that he is not happy after all, and that his appearance of happiness up to this point has been a pretense. He continues to experience feelings of foreboding. He finds his wife, Mildred, in bed listening to earplug radios called "Seashells," just as he has found her every night for the past two years. By her bed, he accidentally kicks an empty bottle of sleeping pills and calls the hospital just as a sonic boom from a squadron of jet bombers shakes the house. Two cynical hospital workers arrive with a machine that pumps Mildred's stomach (Montag later refers to the device as the "Snake") and another that replaces all her poisoned blood with fresh blood. Montag goes outside and listens to the laughter and the voices coming from the brightly lit McClellan house. Montag goes inside again and considers all that has happened to him that night. He feels terribly disoriented as he takes a sleep lozenge and dozes off.

The next day, Mildred remembers nothing about her attempted suicide and denies it when Montag tries to tell her about it. She insists on explaining the plot of the television parlor "family" programs that she watches endlessly on three full-wall screens. Uninterested in her shallow entertainments, Montag leaves for work and finds Clarisse outside walking in the rain, catching raindrops in her mouth—she compares the taste to wine. She rubs a dandelion under her chin and claims that if the pollen rubs off on her, it means she is in love. She rubs it under Montag's chin, but no pollen rubs off, to his embarrassment. She asks him why he chose to be a fireman and says he is unlike the others she has met, who will not talk to her or listen to what she says to them. He tells her to go along to her appointment with her psychiatrist, whom the authorities force her to see due to her supposed lack of "sociability" and her dangerous inclination toward independent thought. After she is gone, he tilts his head back and catches the rain in his mouth for a few moments.

_____

ANALYSIS

Clarisse seems older to Montag than she really is, even older than his wife, who is fourteen years her senior. Mildred seems childish by comparison, perhaps because very little goes through her mind that has not been put there by the vapid television and radio media. Technology has replaced actual human contact for Mildred, just as it has for most of the city's population. She refers to the people on her interactive TV parlor walls (which have been written with one part missing, so that the viewer can read those lines and feel a part of the action on screen) as her "family." She and Montag do not sleep in the same bed, and she seems anxious for him to leave for work in the afternoon.

When Montag comes home from work to find Mildred lying deathlike on the bed, listening to her radio earplugs in the darkness, the room is described as "not empty" and then "indeed empty," because though Mildred is physically there, her thoughts and feelings are elsewhere. Bradbury frequently uses paradoxical phrases, describing a character or thing as dead *and* alive or there *and* not there at once. In Mildred's case, this reflects her empty, half-alive condition. Bradbury uses similar paradoxes to describe the "Snake" stomach pump and, later, the Mechanical Hound.

Although most of the people in Montag's world are completely uninterested in nature, their culture abounds in animal references, such as the mechanical objects called Snake and Hound. The only natural force that people maintain any interest in is fire. However, even fire, once one of the most basic of necessities of human life, has lost its utility and is used primarily for entertainment.

We also see that Mildred's character is more complex than she knows. She suffers from a hidden melancholy that she refuses to accept consciously and that causes her to commit suicide. This same type of repressed inner pain affects much of the population of this world, manifesting itself in self-destructive acts. Montag feels violated by the strangers who come with their machines and take his wife's blood. In this section and throughout the novel, blood is symbolic of a human being's repressed soul or primal, instinctive self—Montag often "feels" his most revolutionary thoughts stirring his blood, and Mildred, who has long lost access to her primal self, remains unchanged when her poisoned blood is replaced with fresh, mechanically administered blood.

The feelings of prescience Montag experiences before meeting Clarisse and before stumbling upon his wife's empty bottle of sleeping pills recur throughout the novel. Bradbury uses such vague premonitions to suggest the inevitability of events. A bit of foreshadowing also takes place in this section and periodically throughout the book, as Montag looks up and contemplates the ventilator grille in his home as though something sinister were hiding in it. Bradbury showcases his rich, poetic prose style early in the novel, starting with the opening paragraph about the pleasures of burning and the extremely detailed, almost scientific digressions about Montag's expectation of seeing someone waiting for him around the corner, and his prescient sense that he is about to kick an object on the floor in his bedroom.

THE HEARTH AND THE SALAMANDER (CONTINUED)

From the first scene in the fire station through burning the old woman on Elm Street

SUMMARY

Montag reaches down to touch the Mechanical Hound in the fire station, and it growls at him and threatens him. Montag tells Captain Beatty what happened and suggests that someone may have set the Hound to react to him like that, since it has threatened him twice before. Montag wonders aloud what the Hound thinks about and pities it when Beatty replies that it thinks only what they tell it to think, of hunting and killing and so forth. The other firemen tease Montag about the Hound, and one tells him about a fireman in Seattle who committed suicide by setting a Hound to his own chemical complex. Beatty assures him no one would have done that to Montag and promises to have the Hound checked out. Over the next week, Montag sees Clarisse outside and talks with her every day. She asks him why he never had any children and tells him that she has stopped going to school because it was mindless and routine. On the eighth day, he does not see Clarisse. He starts to turn back to look for her, but his train arrives and he heads for work. At the firehouse, he asks Beatty what happened to the man whose library they burned the week before. Beatty says he was taken to the insane asylum. Montag wonders aloud what it would have been like to have been in the man's place and almost reveals that he looked at the first line of a book of fairy tales in the library before they burned it.

He asks if firemen ever prevented fires, and two other firemen take out their rule books and show him where it says the Firemen of America were established in 1790 by Benjamin Franklin to burn English-influenced books. Then the alarm sounds, and they head off to a decayed, old house with books hidden in its attic. They push aside an old woman to get to them. A book falls into Montag's hand, and without thinking he hides it beneath his coat. Even after they spray the books with kerosene, the woman refuses to go. Beatty starts to light the fire anyway, but Montag protests and tries to persuade her to leave. She still refuses, and as soon as Montag exits, she strikes a match herself and the house goes up in flames with her in it. The firemen are strangely quiet as they ride back to the station afterward.

ANALYSIS

> So it was the hand that started it all . . . His hands had been infected, and soon it would be his arm. . . . His hands were ravenous.
>
> (See QUOTATIONS, p. 43)

The Mechanical Hound continues the paradoxical theme of living but not Living. Like Mildred and the snakelike machine that pumps her stomach, the Hound is simultaneously like and not like a living thing. It is unlike a real dog in that it is made of metal and has eight legs and a needle in its muzzle that extends and administers a lethal dose of anesthetic. The possibility that someone may have purposely set the Hound's sensors to react hostilely to Montag foreshadows trouble with an enemy in the fire station, as does his interaction with Beatty, who seems to suspect that something is going on with Montag. Montag is conscious of feeling vaguely guilty around Beatty, but he does not know the exact origin of his feeling.

In this section, Montag begins to feel alienated from the other firemen. He realizes suddenly that all the other firemen look exactly like him, with their uniforms, physiques, and grafted-on, sooty smiles. This is simply a physical manifestation of the fact that his society demands that everyone think and act the same. He used to bet with the other firemen on games of releasing animals for the Hound to catch and kill, but now he just lies in his bunk upstairs and listens every night. He begins to question things no other fireman would ever think of, such as why alarms always come in at night, and whether this is simply because fire is prettier then. This explanation makes perfect sense in a society as caught up in superficial aesthetics as Montag's and is in keeping with the novel's portrayal of book burning as a kind of ghoulish entertainment. When the firemen find the old woman still in her house at the scene of the burning, Montag shows a capacity for empathy and compassion that is uncommon in his society. First, he feels highly uncomfortable, since he usually only has to deal with the lifeless books, without human emotions getting involved. Then, though the other men also seem uncomfortable and try to compensate for her silently accusing presence with increased activity and talking, Montag tries to convince her to leave, to save her life.

Beatty's character becomes more complex here as he speaks to the woman. He summarizes his reasons for burning books, saying that none of the books agree with each other and that many are merely subversive lies about people who never actually lived. He compares books—which contain thousands of varying opinions—to the Tower of Babel, the biblical structure that caused the universal human language to be fragmented into thousands of different voices. Beatty recognizes that the comment the old woman made when the firemen arrived was actually a quotation of Hugh Latimer's words to Nicholas Ridley as the two of them were about to be burned at the stake as heretics in sixteenth-century England. This is the first hint of Beatty's impressive knowledge of literature.

The question of individual agency arises again when Montag steals the book. He perceives his crime to be automatic and observes that it involved no thought on his part, that his hands committed the crime on their own. Montag's thoughtless actions here recall Mildred's unconscious overdose; both actions result from a hidden sense of dissatisfaction that neither Mildred nor Montag consciously acknowledges.

THE HEARTH AND THE SALAMANDER
(CONTINUED)

From Montag and Mildred in bed to Beatty's arrival

SUMMARY

Montag goes home and hides the book he has stolen under his pillow. In bed, Mildred suddenly seems very strange and unfamiliar to him as she babbles on about the TV and her TV "family." He gets into his own bed, which is separate from his wife's. He asks her where they first met ten years ago, but neither of them can remember. Mildred gets out of bed and goes to the bathroom to take some sleeping pills, and Montag tries to count the number of times he hears her swallow and wonders if she will forget later and take more. He feels terribly empty and concludes that the TV walls stand between him and his wife. He thinks about her TV "family," with its empty dramas of tenuous connections and transient, sensational images. He tells Mildred he hasn't seen Clarisse for four days and asks if she knows what happened to her. Mildred tells him the family moved away and that she thinks Clarisse was hit by a car and killed.

Montag is sick the next morning, and the omnipresent stink of kerosene makes him vomit. He tells Mildred about burning the old woman and asks her if she would mind if he gave up his job for a while. He tries to make her understand his feelings of guilt at burning the woman and at burning the books, which represent so many people's lives and work, but she will not listen. He baits Mildred by insisting on discussing books and the last time something "bothered" her, but she resists. The argument ends when they see Captain Beatty coming up the front walk.

ANALYSIS

In this section, Montag describes his hands, which he blames for stealing the book, as infected and relates how the "poison" spreads into the rest of his body. This reveals that Montag lacks awareness of his true motivations and that some unconscious force is overpowering his conscious, rational self. Bradbury implies that Montag's defiance and thirst for truth are innate and instinctive but that they have been repressed by a culture that relies on ignorance, complacency, and easy pleasures.

Nonetheless, after stealing the book Montag experiences an intense, disorienting fear. He tries to draw some emotional support from his wife, seeking desperately to remember where they first met. This bit of information takes on a symbolic significance for him as he realizes that he does not truly feel connected to her. Montag is frightened by Mildred's pill-taking habits, but not because he truly cares whether she lives or dies. His fear actually stems from the fact that he doesn't really love her and is trying to avoid acknowledging that fact.

He is moved to tears only when he realizes he would not cry if Mildred overdosed again and died—the true tragedy in his life is the lack of any real feeling. Montag feels that he and his wife are both utterly empty, and he thinks back to Clarisse's dandelion (from the first of "The Hearth and the Salamander") as the sign of his lack of feelings for Mildred. Montag blames the TV walls and various other bits of technological distraction for separating Mildred from him and killing or at least distorting her brain. Bradbury likens Mildred's electronic Seashell thimble to a praying mantis, once again using animal imagery to suggest the voraciousness of their culture's technology. Mildred spends all of her time within her three TV walls and pushes Montag to get her a fourth (which, presumably, would box her in completely). She calls the people on TV her "family" and values their company much more than Montag's. Her life of watching television has destroyed her attention span, and now she can hardly even comprehend what is going on in the programs she watches. Mildred is so disconnected from reality that she forgets to tell Montag that Clarisse was killed and her family moved away; she does not even consider the possibility that this news might upset Montag in any way.

Montag's experience with the old woman has profoundly affected him, and he begins to see everything associated with his job as distasteful and even repugnant. The odor of kerosene now makes him vomit, whereas before he had considered it a "perfume." The Mechanical Hound starts to loom in Montag's imagination as a source of terror. He imagines it lying outside his window in wait for him. (Later we learn that it really has been sent to stalk him.)

Montag realizes for the first time that books are a tangible representation of somebody's entire life and work. He yearns above all for some deeper truth buried beneath his society's layers of lies and transient, vacuous pleasures, and books come to symbolize this truth. However, as Faber later points out, the problem is more fundamental and cannot be solved simply by ending book burning.

SUMMARY & ANALYSIS

THE HEARTH AND THE SALAMANDER
(CONTINUED)

From Beatty's visit through the end of "The Hearth and the Salamander"

SUMMARY

Captain Beatty comes by to check on Montag, saying that he guessed Montag would be calling in sick that day. He tells Montag that every fireman runs into the "problem" he has been experiencing sooner or later, and he relates to him the history of their profession. Beatty's monologue borders on the hysterical, and his tendency to jump from one thing to another without explaining the connection makes his history very hard to follow. Part of the story is that photography, film, and television made it possible to present information in a quickly digestible, visual form, which made the slower, more reflective practice of reading books less popular. Another strand of his argument is that the spread of literacy, and the gigantic increase in the amount of published materials, created pressure for books to be more like one another and easier to read (like *Reader's Digest* condensed books). Finally, Beatty says that "minorities" and special-interest groups found so many things in books objectionable that people finally abandoned debate and started burning books.

Mildred's attention falters while Beatty is talking, and she gets up and begins absentmindedly straightening the room. In doing so, she finds the book behind Montag's pillow and tries to call attention to it, but Montag screams at her to sit down. Beatty pretends not to notice and goes on talking. He explains that eventually the public's demand for uncontroversial, easy pleasure caused printed matter to be diluted to the point that only comic books, trade journals, and sex magazines remained. Beatty explains that after all houses were fireproofed, the firemen's job changed from its old purpose of preventing fires to its new mission of burning the books that could allow one person to excel intellectually, spiritually, and practically over others and so make everyone else feel inferior. Montag asks how someone like Clarisse could exist, and Beatty says the firemen have been keeping an eye on her family because they worked against the schools' system of homogenization. Beatty reveals that he has had a file on the McClellans' odd behaviors for years and says that Clarisse is better off dead.

Beatty urges Montag not to overlook how important he and his fellow firemen are to the happiness of the world. He tells him that every fireman sooner or later becomes curious about books; because he has read some himself, he can assert that they are useless and contradictory. Montag asks what would happen if a fireman accidentally took a book home with him, and Beatty says that he would be allowed to keep it for twenty-four or forty-eight hours, but that the other firemen would then come to burn it if he had not already done so himself. Beatty gets up to leave and asks if Montag will come in to work later. Montag tells him that he may, but he secretly resolves never to go again. After Beatty leaves, Montag tells Mildred that he no longer wants to work at the fire station and shows her a secret stock of about twenty books he has been hiding in the ventilator. In a panic, she tries to burn them, but he stops her. He wants to look at them at least once, and he needs her help. He searches for a reason for his unhappiness in the books, which he has apparently been stealing for some time. Mildred is frightened of them, but Montag is determined to involve her in his search, and he asks for forty-eight hours of support from her to look through the books in hopes of finding something valuable that they can share with others. Someone comes to the door, but they do not answer and he goes away. (Later it is revealed that the Mechanical Hound was the second visitor.) Montag picks up a copy of *Gulliver's Travels* and begins reading.

ANALYSIS

> *We must all be alike. Not everyone born free and equal, as the constitution says, but everyone* MADE *equal. . . . A book is a loaded gun in the house next door. Burn it.*
>
> (See QUOTATIONS, p. 44)

In his explication of the history of book burning, Beatty equates deep thought with sadness, which he rejects as categorically evil. The immediacy of pleasure in this bookless society eliminates thought and, with it, the ability to express sadness, which is why people like Mildred carry around vast amounts of suppressed pain. According to Beatty, mass censorship began with various special-interest groups and minorities clamoring against material they considered offensive, as well as a shrinking attention span in the general populace. As a result, books and ideas were condensed further and further until they were little more than a series of sound bites; they were ultimately eliminated altogether in favor of other, more superficial, sensory-stimulating media. Mass production called for uniformity and effectively eliminated the variance once found in books.

The startling point of Beatty's explanation is that censorship started with the people, not the government (although the government stepped in later in accordance with the people's wishes). Most people stopped reading books long before they were ever burned. It is important to note that Beatty's entire description of the history of the firemen has an oddly ambivalent tone. His speech is filled with irony and sarcasm, and his description of reading strikes the reader as passionate and nostalgic. His championing of book burning, on the other hand, has a perfunctory, insincere tone. Of course, this sarcasm reflects Bradbury's attitude toward what he is writing about, and much of Beatty's complexity stems from the fact that he is simultaneously Bradbury's mouthpiece and villain—everything he says is deliberately ironic.

In the world of shallow hedonists in which Beatty and Montag live, everyone strives to be the same and "intellectual" is a dirty word. Superior minds are persecuted until they fall in line with everyone else. People who are not born equal are *made* equal. Funerals are eliminated because they are a source of unhappiness, death is forgotten as soon as it occurs, and bodies are unceremoniously incinerated. In this society, books are as morbid as corpses, because they contain dead thoughts by dead authors. This society idolizes fire, which represents the easy cleanliness of destruction. As Beatty explains, "Fire is bright and fire is clean."

Beatty also reveals some personal information here, telling Montag that he's tried to understand the universe and knows firsthand its melancholy tendency to make people feel bestial and lonely. He prefers the life of instant pleasure. With this confiding air, Beatty tries to make Montag believe that firemen are essential to the happiness of the world. When Montag's response is to privately assert that he will never be a fireman again, we see how much his resolve and confidence in himself have grown. He is a quite different man from the one who just a short time ago feared that Beatty's skillful rhetoric would convince him to return to work.

The Sieve and the Sand

From the opening through Montag's visit with Faber

Summary

Do you know why books such as this are so
important? Because they have quality. And what does
the word quality mean? To me it means texture. This
book has PORES.

(See QUOTATIONS, *p. 45)*

Montag and Mildred spend the afternoon reading. The Mechanical Hound comes and sniffs at the door. Montag speculates about what it was that made Clarisse so unique. Mildred refuses to talk about someone who is dead and complains that she prefers the people and the pretty colors on her TV walls to books. Montag feels that books must somehow be able to help him out of his ignorance, but he does not understand what he is reading and decides that he must find a teacher. He thinks back to an afternoon a year before when he met an old English professor named Faber in the park. It was apparent that Faber had been reading a book of poetry before Montag arrived. The professor had tried to hide the book and run away, but after Montag reassured him that he was safe, they talked, and Faber gave him his address and phone number. Now Montag calls the professor. He asks him how many copies of the Bible, Shakespeare, or Plato are left in the country. Faber, who thinks Montag is trying to trap him, says none are left and hangs up the phone.

Montag goes back to his pile of books and realizes that he took from the old woman what may be the last copy of the Bible in existence. He considers turning in a substitute to Beatty (who knows he has at least one book), but he realizes that if Beatty knows which book he took, the chief will guess that he has a whole library if he gives him a different book. He decides to have a duplicate made before that night. Mildred tells him that some of her friends are coming over to watch TV with her. Montag, still trying to connect with her, asks her rhetorically if the "family" on TV loves her. She dismisses his question. He takes the subway to Faber's, and on the way tries to memorize verses from the Bible. A jingle for Denham's Dentifrice toothpaste distracts him, and finally he gets up in front of all the passengers and screams at the radio to shut up, waving his book around. The astonished passengers start to call a guard, but Montag gets off at the next stop.

Montag goes to Faber and shows him the book, which alleviates Faber's fear of him, and he asks the old man to teach him to understand what he reads. Faber says that Montag does not know the real reason for his unhappiness and is only guessing that it has something to do with books, since they are the only things he knows for sure are gone. Faber insists that it's not the books themselves that Montag is looking for, but the meaning they contain. The same meaning could be included in existing media like television and radio, but people no longer demand it. Faber compares their superficial society to flowers trying to live on flowers instead of on good, substantive dirt: people are unwilling to accept the basic realities and unpleasant aspects of life.

Faber says that people need quality information, the leisure to digest it, and the freedom to act on what they learn. He defines quality information as a textured and detailed knowledge of life, knowledge of the "pores" on the face of humanity. Faber agrees with Mildred that television seems more "real" than books, but he dislikes it because it is too invasive and controlling. Books at least allow the reader to put them down, giving one time to think and reason about the information they contain.

Montag suggests planting books in the homes of firemen to discredit the profession and see the firehouses burn. Faber doesn't think that this action would get to the heart of the problem, however, lamenting that the firemen aren't really necessary to suppress books because the public stopped reading them of its own accord even before they were burned. Faber says they just need to be patient, since the coming war will eventually mean the death of the TV families. Montag concludes that they could use that as a chance to bring books back.

Montag bullies Faber out of his cowardice by tearing pages out of the precious Bible one by one, and Faber finally agrees to help, revealing that he knows someone with a printing press who used to print his college newspaper. Montag asks for help with Beatty that night, and Faber gives him a two-way radio he has created that will fit in Montag's ear; that way the professor can hear what Beatty has to say and also prompt Montag. Montag decides to risk giving Beatty a substitute book, and Faber agrees to see his printer friend.

ANALYSIS

Mildred's refusal to talk about Clarisse because she is dead indicates her denial of death, a denial that characterizes society as a whole. This denial is related to the widespread ignorance of history and fear of books, because history and books connect readers to the dead. In contrast, Montag feels a kind of wonder that the books written by dead people somehow remind him of Clarisse. He openly accepts and ponders death, telling Faber that his wife is dying and that a friend of his is already dead, along with someone who might have been a friend (meaning the old woman). Mildred still does not see any possible advantage in reading and is angered by the danger Montag puts her in, asking if she is not more important than a Bible. Montag hopes that reading will help him understand the mistakes that have led the world into two atomic wars since 1990 and that have made the rest of the world hate his country for its narcissistic hedonism.

Faber becomes a more important character in this section. Faber may have planted the seed of Montag's inner revolution the year before in the park, when he told the fireman that he does not talk about things but rather the meanings of things, and therefore he knows he is alive. This theme of deeper meanings being necessary for life is central to the book. And although Montag knew he had a book in his pocket, Faber gave him his address anyway, allowing Montag to choose whether to befriend him or turn him in. When Montag visits Faber, he tells the professor that he just wants someone to listen to him talk until he starts to make sense. He acknowledges his own ignorance, which demonstrates his increasing self-awareness, and hopes to learn from Faber.

Although Faber is a strong moral voice in the novel, his self-professed flaw of cowardice is also introduced in this section. He is reluctant to risk helping Montag and finally agrees to do so only by means of his audio transmitter, hiding behind this device while Montag risks his life.

Montag's newfound resolve is also fragile at this point in the novel. He expresses concern that Beatty will be able to persuade him to return to his former life. Montag imagines Beatty describing the burning pages of a book as black butterflies, an image that recalls Montag's own joy at the metamorphosis enacted by fire in the opening paragraph of the book.

An important symbol is expressed in the title of this section, "The Sieve and the Sand," which comes from Montag's childhood memory of trying to fill a sieve with sand on the beach to get a dime from a mischievous cousin and crying at the futility of the task. He compares this memory to his attempt to read the whole Bible as quickly as possible on the subway in the hope that, if he reads fast enough, some of the material will stay in his memory. The sand is symbolic of the tangible truth Montag seeks and the sieve of the human mind seeking truth. Truth is elusive and, the metaphor suggests, impossible to grasp in any permanent way.

The Sieve and the Sand (continued)

From after Montag's visit with Faber through the end of "The Sieve and the Sand"

Summary

Montag withdraws money from his account to give to Faber and listens to reports over the radio that the country is mobilizing for war. Faber reads to him from the Book of Job over the two-way radio in his ear. He goes home, and two of Mildred's friends, Mrs. Phelps and Mrs. Bowles, arrive and promptly disappear into the TV parlor. Montag turns off the TV walls and tries to engage the three women in conversation. They reluctantly oblige him, but he becomes angry when they describe how they voted in the last presidential election, based solely on the physical appearance and other superficial qualities of the candidates. Their detached and cynical references to their families and the impending war angers him further. He brings out a book of poetry and shows it to them, despite their objections and Faber's (delivered via his ear radio). Mildred quickly concocts a lie, explaining that a fireman is allowed to bring home one book a year to show to his family and prove what nonsense books are. Faber orders Montag to take the escape route Mildred has provided by agreeing with her.

Refusing to be deterred, Montag reads the women "Dover Beach" by Matthew Arnold. Mrs. Phelps, who has just told everyone quite casually about her husband's departure for the oncoming war, bursts into tears, and Mrs. Bowles declares the cause to be the evil, emotional messiness of poetry. She denounces Montag for reading it. Montag drops the book into the incinerator at Faber's prompting. He yells at Mrs. Bowles to go home and think about her empty life, and both women leave. Mildred disappears into the bedroom. Montag discovers that she has been burning the books one by one, and he rehides them in the backyard. Montag feels guilty for upsetting Mildred's friends and wonders if they are right in focusing only on pleasure. Faber tells him that he would agree if there were no war and all was right with the world, but that those realities call for attention.

Montag heads off to the fire station, and Faber both scolds and consoles him on the way. Montag hands his book over to Beatty, who throws it into the trashcan without even looking at the title and welcomes him back after his period of folly. Beatty browbeats Montag with a storm of literary quotations to confuse him and convince him that books are better burned than read. Montag is so afraid of making a mistake with Beatty that he cannot move his feet. Faber tells him not to be afraid of mistakes, as they sharpen the mind. An alarm comes through, and Beatty glances at the address and takes the wheel of the fire engine. They arrive at their destination, and Montag sees that it is his own house.

<hr />

ANALYSIS

Bradbury uses several significant religious references in this section to illuminate Montag's process of self-realization. First, Faber reads from the Book of Job, a part of the Bible in which God and Satan make a wager about whether Job will remain faithful to God when subjected to terrible afflictions. Clearly, Faber encourages Montag to endure despite the difficulty of his undertaking. Montag, however, is becoming so tired of mindlessly doing what other people say that he becomes suspicious of Faber's orders, and Faber in turn praises him for his development of independent thought.

Next, Montag compares Mildred's friends to religious objects, based on the fact that he can't understand such objects any more than he can Mildred's friends. The two women seem artificial, superficial, and empty to Montag. The conversation that Montag forces them to have reveals their lack of concern about the coming war, the pervasiveness and casual treatment of suicide in their society, and the deplorable state of family ethics. They remind him of icons he once saw in a church and did not understand; they seem strange and meaningless to him.

In a third instance of religious imagery, Faber describes himself as water and Montag as fire, claiming that the merging of the two will produce wine. Jesus Christ's transformation of water into wine was one of the miracles that proved his identity and instilled faith in people. Montag longs to confirm his own identity through a similar self-transformation. He hopes that when he becomes this new self, he will be able to look back and understand the man he used to be.

Montag opens his book of poetry to "Dover Beach," which is quite appropriate to his circumstances, as it deals with the theme of lost faith, and of the capacity for personal relationships to replace faith. The poem also deals with the emptiness of life's promises and the unthinking violence of war. Shortly afterward, Montag has a Shakespearean moment, when he returns to the fire station and compulsively washes his hands in an attempt to clear his guilt, feeling they are "gloved in blood"—a clear reference to Lady Macbeth.

Montag's impressionability is clear in this section, and Faber's voice in his ear begins to spur him to bold actions. When Montag gives in to Faber's command to agree with Mildred, the narrator describes his mouth as having "moved like Faber's"; he has become Faber's mouthpiece. After only a short time with the audio transmitter in his ear, Montag feels that he has known Faber a lifetime and that Faber has actually become a part of him. Faber tries to act as a wise, cautious brain within Montag's young, reckless body. Here again, Bradbury illustrates the contradictory nature of technology—it is both positive and negative, simultaneously beneficial and manipulative.

Bradbury further develops the opposition between Faber and Beatty in this section. Beatty seems vaguely satanic, as if he and Faber are fighting over Montag's very soul. When Montag returns to the fire station, Beatty spouts learned quotations like mad and uses literature to justify banning literature. He hints again at similarities between himself and Montag, saying that he has been through Montag's phase and warning that a little knowledge can be dangerous without further knowledge to temper the revolutionary spirit it produces. Faber tells Montag to consider Beatty's argument and then hear his, and to decide for himself which side to follow. Here he lets Montag make his own decision and stops ordering him around. Beatty's use of literature against Montag is brilliant; this is obviously the most powerful weapon he has against Montag's doubts.

BURNING BRIGHT

From the opening through the second visit with Faber

SUMMARY

Montag gazes at Clarisse's empty house, and Beatty, guessing that he has fallen under her influence, berates him for it. Mildred rushes out of the house with a suitcase and is driven away in a taxi, and

Montag realizes she must have called in the alarm. Beatty orders Montag to burn the house by himself with his flamethrower and warns that the Hound is on the watch for him if he tries to escape. Montag burns everything, and when he is finished, Beatty places him under arrest.

Beatty sees that Montag is listening to something and strikes him on the head. The radio falls out of Montag's ear, and Beatty picks it up, saying that he will have it traced to find the person on the other end. After Beatty eggs him on with more literary quotations, his last a quote from *Julius Caesar*, Montag turns his flamethrower on Beatty and burns him to a crisp. The other firemen do not move, and he knocks them out. The Mechanical Hound appears and injects Montag's leg with anesthetic before he manages to destroy it with his flamethrower. Montag stumbles away on his numb leg. He goes to where he hid the books in his backyard and finds four that Mildred missed. He hears sirens approaching and tries to continue down the alley, but he falls and begins to sob. He forces himself to rise and runs until the numbness leaves his leg. Montag puts a regular Seashell radio in his ear and hears a police alert warning people to be on the lookout for him, that he is alone and on foot.

He finds a gas station and washes the soot off his face so he will look less suspicious. He hears on the radio that war has been declared. He starts to cross a wide street and is nearly hit by a car speeding toward him. At first, Montag thinks it is the police coming to get him, but he later realizes the car's passengers are children who would have killed him for no reason at all, and he wonders angrily whether they were the motorists who killed Clarisse. He creeps into one of his coworkers' houses and hides the books, then calls in an alarm from a phone booth. He goes to Faber's house, tells him what has happened, and gives the professor some money. Faber instructs him to follow the old railroad tracks out of town to look for camps of homeless intellectuals and tells Montag to meet him in St. Louis sometime in the future, where he is going to meet a retired printer. Faber turns on the TV news, and they hear that a new Mechanical Hound, followed by a helicopter camera crew, has been sent out after Montag. Montag takes a suitcase full of Faber's old clothes, tells the professor how to purge his house of Montag's scent so the Hound will not be led there, and runs off into the night. Faber plans to take a bus out of the city to visit his printer friend as soon as possible.

ANALYSIS

> *It's perpetual motion; the thing man wanted to invent
> but never did . . . It's a mystery. . . . Its real beauty is
> that it destroys responsibility and consequences . . .
> clean, quick, sure; nothing to rot later. Antibiotic,
> aesthetic, practical.*
>
> *(See* QUOTATIONS, *p. 46)*

Mildred's betrayal of Montag is complete, and he realizes that she will soon forget him as she drives away, consoling herself with her Seashell radio. Montag does not feel particularly angry at her, however; his feelings for her are only pity and regret.

This part of the novel is dominated by the final confrontation between Montag and Beatty. Beatty's ironic self-awareness, his understanding that his choices have not made him truly happy, seems to grow throughout the novel, and it comes to the surface in his final scene, when his behavior seems deliberately calculated to result in his own death.

Montag remains emotionally detached in this section. He enjoys burning his own house as much as he enjoyed burning those of others, and he begins to agree with Beatty that fire is removing his problems. He imagines Mildred and his whole previous life under the ashes, and feels that he is really far away and that his body is dead. Moreover, he claims that it is not exactly he who commits Beatty's murder—he cannot tell if it's his hands or Beatty's reaction to them that spurs him to the act. Beatty is described as no longer human and no longer known to Montag when he catches fire. Again, like so many other things in the novel, fire has two contradictory meanings at once. It represents Montag's subjugation and his liberation, and he achieves his final emancipation by abusing its power. Murder is, after all, a far worse crime than book burning. Only later does Montag acknowledge what he has done and feel some remorse for his actions.

Montag is not as different from Mildred, Beatty, and others as he thinks. In this section, he confides in Faber that he has been going around all his life doing one thing and feeling another, an unconscious dualism that resembles the conflicted psyches of Mildred and Beatty. Also, when he and Faber watch the sensationalist TV news coverage of his escape and the chase, the possibility of watching the unfolding drama on TV fascinates Montag, and he finds all the glitz and tabloid glamour he has inspired somewhat flattering. If he is killed on TV, he wonders if he could sum up his whole life in a few words in the brief moments before his death so as to make an impact on the people watching. Montag has not yet escaped from the culture against which he revolts—he is still concerned, even in his most dire moment, with surface appearances, fame, and sensationalism. However, the last image at Faber's house suggests a hopeful end for Montag and his world: it is of rain (from the sprinklers), countering the images of fire associated with the men pursuing Montag.

Bradbury's writing style is particularly poetic in this section. He uses figurative language extensively (especially stage and circus metaphors) and often bends the rules of grammar, using sentence fragments as transitional devices and one lengthy sentence to convey the breathlessness of Montag's flight.

BURNING BRIGHT (CONTINUED)

From after leaving Faber's through the death of the fake Montag

SUMMARY

Montag is able to watch the Hound track him by glancing through people's house windows into their TV parlors. Literally everybody is watching the televised chase. Montag sees the Hound hesitate when it gets to Faber's house, but it quickly runs on. As Montag continues to run toward the river, he hears an announcement on his Seashell radio telling everyone to get up and look out their doors and windows for him on the count of ten. He reaches the river just as the announcer counts to ten and all the doors in the neighborhood start to open. To keep the Hound from picking up his scent, he wades into the river and drifts away with the current. He avoids the searchlights of the police helicopters, and then sees them turn and fly away. He washes ashore in the countryside. Stepping out of the river, he is overwhelmed by the sights, sounds, and smells of nature. He finds the railroad track and follows it. As he walks, he senses strongly that Clarisse once walked there, too.

The track leads him to a fire with five men sitting around it. The leader of the men sees him in the shadows and invites him to join them, introducing himself as Granger. Granger reveals a portable TV set and tells him that they have been watching the chase and expecting him to come. The men at the fire, though homeless, are surprisingly neat and clean, and have considerable technology. Granger gives Montag a bottle of colorless fluid to drink and explains that it will change the chemical index of his perspiration so the Hound will not be able to find him. Granger tells him the search has continued in the opposite direction and that the police will be looking for a scapegoat to save themselves from the humiliation of losing their prey. The men gather around the TV to watch as the camera zooms in on a man walking down the street, smoking a cigarette. The announcer identifies this man as Montag. The Hound appears and pounces on him, and the announcer declares that Montag is dead and a crime against society has been avenged. The homeless men reflect that the police probably chose the man to be their scapegoat because of his habit of walking by himself—clearly a dangerous and antisocial habit.

ANALYSIS

> The sun burnt every day. It burnt Time . . . Time
> was busy burning the years and the people anyway,
> without any help from him. So if HE burnt things with
> the firemen and the sun burnt Time, that meant that
> EVERYTHING burnt!
>
> *(See* QUOTATIONS, *p. 46)*

Bradbury uses several devices to heighten the tension of the chase sequence, including the use of dramatic pauses (such as when the Hound pauses on Faber's lawn), the description of the Hound's progress from Montag's perspective, and the countdown to the "look-out" in which everybody is to open their doors. This latter device effectively pits the entire city against Montag and creates a definite time factor (as opposed to the progress of the Hound, which is an undetermined distance away from Montag). Montag has to make an effort to remember that he is not watching a fictional drama but his own life unfolding on twenty million TV screens.

Montag leaves the frightening unreality of the city, which he thinks of as a stage of actors and a séance of ghosts, and enters the world of the countryside, which feels equally unreal to him because of its newness. Drifting peacefully down the river into darkness, Montag finally experiences the quiet and freedom that he needs to think.

Montag considers the moon, which in turn reminds him of the sun and then of fire. He concludes that the sun actually burns time, scorching away the years and all the people on the planet. This is a puzzling statement, but it means simply that time, represented by the rising and setting of the sun, will inevitably destroy people and everything they have worked for. He realizes that if he continues to burn things as he has all his life, everything worthwhile will be destroyed even more quickly. He begins to think of his life as having a different purpose, of using his life to preserve rather than destroy. Soon after he has these thoughts, he sees the flame that the hobos warm their hands over. For the first time in his life, he discovers that fire can sustain life as well as destroy it.

As he contemplates the silence of the countryside, Montag's thoughts turn to Mildred. He realizes she would not be able to tolerate the silence and is saddened at the thought. In contrast, Montag feels increasingly comfortable in the presence of nature, becoming "fully aware of his entire body." He no longer feels that his mind, hands, and blood are separate entities, as he did in the city. Montag becomes a whole person for the first time.

Burning Bright (continued)

From after the fake Montag's death through the end of the novel

Summary

After witnessing the anonymous scapegoat's death on the television, Granger turns to Montag and ironically remarks, "Welcome back to life." He introduces Montag to the other men, who are all former professors and intellectuals. He tells Montag that they have perfected a method of recalling word-for-word anything that they have read once. Each one of them has a different classic stored in his memory. Granger explains that they are part of a network of thousands of people all over the country who have bits and pieces of different books stored within their memories. Granger says that Montag is important because he represents their "back-up copy" of the Book of Ecclesiastes. Finally, Montag's reading has been validated by someone.

Granger says that his group is waiting for humanity to become ready for books again so that they can be of some use to the world. He says that the most important thing they have to remember is that they are not important in themselves, but only as repositories of knowledge. Granger says they are prepared to wait for as long as it takes and will pass their books down through succeeding generations if need be. He accepts the possibility that someday there will be another Dark Age and they will have to go through it all again, but he is confident about man's determination to save what is worth saving. They put out the fire and walk downstream in the darkness.

Montag searches the other men's faces for some glow of resolve or glint of hidden knowledge, but he is disappointed. Seeing this, the men laugh and tell him not to judge a book by its cover. Montag tells them that he left his wife back in the city and worries aloud that something must be wrong with him, because he does not miss her and would not be sad if she were killed. Granger tells him a story about the death of his grandfather, stressing that his grandfather, a sculptor, was a man who "*did* things to the world." Granger believes that when people change even a small part of the world thoughtfully and deliberately, they leave behind enough of their souls to enable other people to mourn them properly.

Suddenly, they see jets flash over the city and drop their bombs; the city is vaporized by the explosion. The men are knocked flat by the shock wave. As he clings to the earth, Montag mentally pictures Mildred just as she's about to meet her death. He suddenly remembers that he met her in Chicago. Afterward, Montag thinks of the Book of Ecclesiastes and repeats it to himself. The aftershock dies down, and the men rise and eat breakfast. Granger compares mankind to a phoenix rising again and again from its own ashes, and comments that they will first need to build a mirror factory to take a long look at themselves. The men turn upriver toward the city to help the survivors rebuild from the ashes.

ANALYSIS

Granger's ironic welcoming of Montag back from the dead symbolizes Montag's rebirth into a more meaningful life. Bradbury employs butterfly imagery throughout the book, specifically to describe the "death" of burning books, so the idea of metamorphosis or transformation has been foreshadowed. The fact that the men can recover every word of books they have read makes them living conduits to the dead. They playfully identify themselves to Montag by the names of long-dead authors. The traces of the past contained in books offer these men multiple lives, identities, and opportunities for rebirth. In this new life, Montag has the three things that Faber told him were required for a full life: exposure to nature and the world of books, leisure to think, and freedom to act.

When Montag sees the enemy bombers, his thoughts turn to the people he has lost: Clarisse, Faber, and Mildred. When the bombs obliterate the city, he suddenly remembers that he met Mildred in Chicago, suggesting that he has somehow managed to feel the connection that was missing when she was alive. Granger's story about his grandfather, with its moral about the importance of leaving one's mark on the world, resonates with Montag's desire to leave a meaningful legacy. From the beginning of the novel he has been growing increasingly dissatisfied with a life based on empty pleasures and devoid of real connections to other people. Montag looks back at the city and realizes that he gave it only ashes.

Granger compares mankind to the phoenix, a mythological creature that is consumed by fire only to rise from its own ashes in a cycle that it repeats eternally. He suggests that man's advantage over the phoenix is his ability to recognize when he has made a mistake, so that eventually he will learn not to repeat it. Remembering the mistakes of the past is the task that Granger and his group have set for themselves. They believe that the collective memory represented by books is the key to mankind's survival, and that this shared culture is more important than any individual.

At the end of the novel, Granger remarks that they should build a mirror factory so mankind can look at itself. This recalls Montag's description of Clarisse as a mirror in the beginning of "The Hearth and the Salamander." Mirrors are a symbol of self-understanding, of seeing oneself clearly. They can also multiply and propagate images, as reading and memorizing books multiplies the identities and lives of Granger and the others.

As they walk upriver to find survivors, Montag knows they will eventually talk, and he tries to remember passages from the Bible appropriate to the occasion. He brings to mind Ecclesiastes 3:1, "To everything there is a season," and also Revelations 22:2, "And on either side of the river was there a tree of life . . . and the leaves of the tree were for the healing of the nations," which he decides to save for when they reach the city. The verse from Revelations refers to the holy city of God, and the last line of the book, "When we reach the city," implies a strong symbolic connection between the atomic holocaust of Montag's world and the Apocalypse of the Bible.

IMPORTANT QUOTATIONS EXPLAINED

1. So it was the hand that started it all . . . His hands had been infected, and soon it would be his arms . . . His hands were ravenous.

This passage from "The Hearth and the Salamander" refers to Montag's theft of books from the old woman's house. Montag guiltily portrays his actions as an involuntary bodily reflex. He describes his crime as automatic and claims it involves no thought on his part. He blames his hands for several other crimes in the course of the book, and they become a powerful symbol for Montag's instincts of rebellion, will, and moral imperative. Montag's thoughtless actions here are akin to Mildred's unconscious overdose, as they are the result of some hidden sense of dissatisfaction within him that he does not consciously acknowledge.

Montag regards his hands as infected from stealing the book and describes how the "poison works its way into the rest of his body." Montag uses the word "poison" to refer to his strong sense of guilt and wrongdoing. Later, the novel incorporates a reference to Shakespeare, as Montag compulsively washes his hands at the fire station in an attempt to cleanse his guilt. His feeling they are "gloved in blood" is a clear reference to Lady Macbeth. Montag's hands function as a symbol of defiance and thirst for truth.

2. We must all be alike. Not everyone born free and equal, as
    the constitution says, but everyone *made* equal . . . A book
    is a loaded gun in the house next door. Burn it. Take the
    shot from the weapon. Breach man's mind.

Captain Beatty speaks these lines toward the end of "The Hearth
and the Salamander" while explaining the revisionist history of firemen to Montag in his home. It is important to note that Beatty's
whole speech has an ironic sound. He defends the disintegration of
authenticity in a passionate, almost regretful tone. He is willing to
defend the "equalization" of society while still remaining educated
himself, and denounces the use of books as weapons while freely
using them that way himself. Because of these ambiguities, Beatty is
the most complex character in the book, and he uses his book-edu-
cated mind, his "loaded gun," to manipulate Montag mercilessly.
One wonders, as Faber does, if he chose his job after a fall from faith
in books, as he claims, or to enable himself to gain legal access to
books through his position of authority.

3. Do you know why books such as this are so important?
    Because they have quality. And what does the word quality
    mean? To me it means texture. This book has *pores*.

QUOTATIONS

Faber speaks these words to Montag toward the beginning of "The
Sieve and the Sand," as he explains the importance of books. Faber
tells Montag that it's not the books themselves that Montag is looking for, but the meaning they contain. The same meaning could be
included in existing media like television and radio, but people no
longer demand it. According to Faber, Montag is really in search of
"quality," which the professor defines as "texture"—the details of
life, that is, authentic experience. People need quality information,
the leisure to digest it, and the freedom to act on what has been
learned. Faber's comment that a book has "pores" also evokes the
sieve in the title "The Sieve and the Sand." Trying to fill your mind
by reading books is like trying to fill a leaking bucket, because the
words slip from your memory before you can even finish reading
anything.

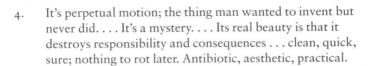

4.   It's perpetual motion; the thing man wanted to invent but
     never did. . . . It's a mystery. . . . Its real beauty is that it
     destroys responsibility and consequences . . . clean, quick,
     sure; nothing to rot later. Antibiotic, aesthetic, practical.

Beatty speaks these lines to Montag outside Montag's home in
"Burning Bright," right before Montag burns him to death with
the flamethrower. He muses about the mystical nature of fire, its
unexplained beauty, and the fascination it holds for people. With
characteristic irony, Beatty, who has just accused Montag of not
considering the consequences of his actions, then defines the beauty
of fire as its ability to destroy consequences and responsibilities.
What he describes is very nearly a cult of fire, a fitting depiction
of their society's devotion to cleanliness and destruction. Unfortu-
nately, Montag turns Beatty's philosophy against him by turning
the flamethrower on his boss, inflicting an "antibiotic, aesthetic,
practical" death.

5.   The sun burnt every day. It burnt Time . . . Time was busy
     burning the years and the people anyway, without any help
     from him. So if *he* burnt things with the firemen and the
     sun burnt Time, that meant that *everything* burnt!

In this passage, Montag muses on the sun as he escapes the city and
floats down the river in "Burning Bright." Montag sees the stars for
the first time in years, and he finally enjoys the leisure to think that
Faber told him he would need in order to regain his life. He starts by
considering the moon, which gets its light from the sun, then considers that the sun is akin to time and burns with its own fire. If the
sun burns time (and, thus, burns away the years and the people) and
he and the firemen continue to burn, everything will burn. These
thoughts lead him to the conclusion that since the sun will not stop
burning, he and the firemen must stop. In these lines, Bradbury repeats the word "burning" to communicate the sense of revelation
that Montag experiences as he considers this and to subtly suggest
that the ex-fireman must now redefine his ingrained conceptions of
fire and burning, and, therefore, his identity and purpose.

QUOTATIONS

KEY FACTS

FULL TITLE
Fahrenheit 451

AUTHOR
Ray Bradbury

TYPE OF WORK
Novel

GENRE
Science fiction

LANGUAGE
English

TIME AND PLACE WRITTEN
1950–1953, Los Angeles, California

DATE OF FIRST PUBLICATION
1953 (a shorter version entitled "The Fireman" was published in 1951 in *Galaxy Science Fiction*)

PUBLISHER
Ballantine Books

NARRATOR
Third-person, limited omniscient; follows Montag's point of view, often articulating his interior monologues

CLIMAX
Montag's murder of Beatty

PROTAGONIST
Montag

ANTAGONIST
Beatty, but also society in general

SETTING (TIME)
Sometime in the twenty-fourth century; there have been two atomic wars since 1990

SETTING (PLACE)
In and around an unspecified city

POINT OF VIEW
Montag's

FALLING ACTION
Montag's trip out of the city into the country

TENSE
Past, with occasional transitions into present tense during Montag's interior monologues and stream-of-consciousness passages

FORESHADOWING
Montag's uncanny feelings of prescience; early descriptions of the Mechanical Hound; Montag's nervous glances toward the ventilator shaft where he has hidden his books; discussion of the qualities of fire

TONE
Foreboding and menacing, disoriented, poetic, bitterly satirical

THEMES
Censorship, knowledge versus ignorance

MOTIFS
Paradoxes, animals and nature, religion, television and radio

SYMBOLS
Fire, blood, the Electric-Eyed Snake, the hearth, the salamander, the phoenix, the sieve and the sand, Denham's Dentifrice, the dandelion, mirrors

STUDY QUESTIONS

1. *How plausible is the future envisioned in this novel? Specifically, do you think the author provides a convincing account of how censorship became so rampant in this society?*

As noted in the analysis of the "Censorship" theme (in "Themes, Motifs & Symbols"), the future envisioned in this novel is brought about by many different factors that may or may not relate directly to censorship. This society is characterized by fast cars, violent youth, invasive television programming, intolerant special-interest groups, and so on. To answer this question effectively, the reader first has to combine a number of these fragmented factors to form the best explanation of this future that he or she can—Bradbury doesn't make the connections for us. Then the reader would have to evaluate this explanation by weighing the individual factors. For instance, does it seem accurate to say that special-interest groups exert a great deal of pressure for writers to conform to one norm? Do television and youth culture really threaten to supplant reading?

2. *Why do you think Beatty hates books?*

It is obvious that Beatty has spent a considerable portion of his life not just reading but passionately absorbed in books. His facility with literary quotations by itself demonstrates this. The first place to look for an answer to this question is in his statements to Montag about why books are dangerous and worthless. For example, he tells Montag that books do not give definite answers, that they contradict themselves and one another, and that different people can "use" them to make absolutely contradictory points. Generalizing from these statements, we can infer that he has become frustrated with books because they don't have one stable meaning. They are too complex and can be interpreted in multiple ways, so nobody can really be said to have mastered them. Beatty may dislike books because he wants to be the one in control of the answers. This inference can be connected to the major theme of "The Sieve and the Sand": the process of reading may be likened to a person trying to fill a bucket that has holes in its bottom; it may be frustrating and does not guarantee the reader access to a tangible meaning. While the sieve and sand image is used to describe the frustrations Montag experiences, it might provide clues to Beatty's frustrations as well.

3.   Read the poem "Dover Beach," by Matthew Arnold.
     In what ways is it significant that Montag reads this
     particular poem to Mildred and her friends?

The speaker in "Dover Beach" relates that his world used to be filled
with and surrounded by faith, like an ocean (the "sea of faith"), but
that this sea has receded, and faith has abandoned his world. There
are many ways to interpret the speaker's statement, but one fairly
definite meaning is that the speaker has lost the religious belief that
used to sustain him. He tells the woman he is speaking to that they
must cling to one another, because all that they have now that faith
has abandoned the world is each other. The reader should be able to
relate this much of the poem to the novel by comparing the world
of the novel with the world of the poem. Is the world of the novel a
world that has been abandoned by faith? What would that mean?
Next, the reader should ask whether there is a corollary between the
couple in the poem and the world of the novel. Is Montag asking his
wife for something similar to what the speaker in "Dover Beach"
asks for? Is he likely to get it from Mildred, or from any of these
women? Why or why not?

How to Write Literary Analysis

The Literary Essay: A Step-by-Step Guide

When you read for pleasure, your only goal is enjoyment. You might find yourself reading to get caught up in an exciting story, to learn about an interesting time or place, or just to pass time. Maybe you're looking for inspiration, guidance, or a reflection of your own life. There are as many different, valid ways of reading a book as there are books in the world.

When you read a work of literature in an English class, however, you're being asked to read in a special way: you're being asked to perform *literary analysis*. To analyze something means to break it down into smaller parts and then examine how those parts work, both individually and together. Literary analysis involves examining all the parts of a novel, play, short story, or poem—elements such as character, setting, tone, and imagery—and thinking about how the author uses those elements to create certain effects.

A literary essay isn't a book review: you're not being asked whether or not you liked a book or whether you'd recommend it to another reader. A literary essay also isn't like the kind of book report you wrote when you were younger, where your teacher wanted you to summarize the book's action. A high school- or college-level literary essay asks, "How does this piece of literature actually work?" "How does it do what it does?" and, "Why might the author have made the choices he or she did?"

The Seven Steps

No one is born knowing how to analyze literature; it's a skill you learn and a process you can master. As you gain more practice with this kind of thinking and writing, you'll be able to craft a method that works best for you. But until then, here are seven basic steps to writing a well-constructed literary essay:

1. *Ask questions*
2. *Collect evidence*
3. *Construct a thesis*

4. Develop and organize arguments
5. Write the introduction
6. Write the body paragraphs
7. Write the conclusion

---

1. ASK QUESTIONS

When you're assigned a literary essay in class, your teacher will often provide you with a list of writing prompts. Lucky you! Now all you have to do is choose one. Do yourself a favor and pick a topic that interests you. You'll have a much better (not to mention easier) time if you start off with something you enjoy thinking about. If you are asked to come up with a topic by yourself, though, you might start to feel a little panicked. Maybe you have too many ideas—or none at all. Don't worry. Take a deep breath and start by asking yourself these questions:

- **What struck you?** Did a particular image, line, or scene linger in your mind for a long time? If it fascinated you, chances are you can draw on it to write a fascinating essay.

- **What confused you?** Maybe you were surprised to see a character act in a certain way, or maybe you didn't understand why the book ended the way it did. Confusing moments in a work of literature are like a loose thread in a sweater: if you pull on it, you can unravel the entire thing. Ask yourself why the author chose to write about that character or scene the way he or she did and you might tap into some important insights about the work as a whole.

- **Did you notice any patterns?** Is there a phrase that the main character uses constantly or an image that repeats throughout the book? If you can figure out how that pattern weaves through the work and what the significance of that pattern is, you've almost got your entire essay mapped out.

- **Did you notice any contradictions or ironies?** Great works of literature are complex; great literary essays recognize and explain those complexities. Maybe the title (*Happy Days*) totally disagrees with the book's subject matter (hungry orphans dying in the woods). Maybe the main character acts one way around his family and a completely different way around his friends and associates. If you can find a way to explain a work's contradictory elements, you've got the seeds of a great essay.

At this point, you don't need to know exactly what you're going to say about your topic; you just need a place to begin your exploration. You can help direct your reading and brainstorming by formulating your topic as a *question,* which you'll then try to answer in your essay. The best questions invite critical debates and discussions, not just a rehashing of the summary. Remember, you're looking for something you can *prove or argue* based on evidence you find in the text. Finally, remember to keep the scope of your question in mind: is this a topic you can adequately address within the word or page limit you've been given? Conversely, is this a topic big enough to fill the required length?

GOOD QUESTIONS

"Are Romeo and Juliet's parents responsible for the deaths of their children?"
"Why do pigs keep showing up in LORD OF THE FLIES*?"*
"Are Dr. Frankenstein and his monster alike? How?"

BAD QUESTIONS

"What happens to Scout in TO KILL A MOCKINGBIRD*?"*
"What do the other characters in JULIUS CAESAR *think about Caesar?"*
"How does Hester Prynne in THE SCARLET LETTER *remind me of my sister?"*

---

2. COLLECT EVIDENCE

Once you know what question you want to answer, it's time to scour the book for things that will help you answer the question. Don't worry if you don't know what you want to say yet—right now you're just collecting ideas and material and letting it all percolate. Keep track of passages, symbols, images, or scenes that deal with your topic. Eventually, you'll start making connections between these examples and your thesis will emerge.

Here's a brief summary of the various parts that compose each and every work of literature. These are the elements that you will analyze in your essay, and which you will offer as evidence to support your arguments. For more on the parts of literary works, see the Glossary of Literary Terms at the end of this section.

ELEMENTS OF STORY   These are the *what*s of the work—what happens, where it happens, and to whom it happens.

- **Plot:** All of the events and actions of the work.

- **Character:** The people who act and are acted upon in a literary work. The main character of a work is known as the *protagonist.*

- **Conflict:** The central tension in the work. In most cases, the protagonist wants something, while opposing forces (antagonists) hinder the protagonist's progress.

- **Setting:** When and where the work takes place. Elements of setting include location, time period, time of day, weather, social atmosphere, and economic conditions.

- **Narrator:** The person telling the story. The narrator may straightforwardly report what happens, convey the subjective opinions and perceptions of one or more characters, or provide commentary and opinion in his or her own voice.

- **Themes:** The main idea or message of the work—usually an abstract idea about people, society, or life in general. A work may have many themes, which may be in tension with one another.

ELEMENTS OF STYLE   These are the *how*s—how the characters speak, how the story is constructed, and how language is used throughout the work.

- **Structure and organization:** How the parts of the work are assembled. Some novels are narrated in a linear, chronological fashion, while others skip around in time. Some plays follow a traditional three- or five-act structure, while others are a series of loosely connected scenes. Some authors deliberately leave gaps in their works, leaving readers to puzzle out the missing information. A work's structure and organization can tell you a lot about the kind of message it wants to convey.

- **Point of view:** The perspective from which a story is told. In *first-person point of view*, the narrator involves him or herself in the story. ("I went to the store"; "We watched in horror as the bird slammed into the window.") A first-person narrator is usually the protagonist of the work, but not always. In *third-person point of view*, the narrator does not participate in the story. A third-person narrator may closely follow a specific character, recounting that individual character's thoughts or experiences, or it may be what we call an *omniscient* narrator. Omniscient narrators see and know all: they can witness any event in any time or place and are privy to the inner thoughts and feelings of all characters. Remember that the narrator and the author are not the same thing!

- **Diction:** Word choice. Whether a character uses dry, clinical language or flowery prose with lots of exclamation points can tell you a lot about his or her attitude and personality.

- **Syntax:** Word order and sentence construction. Syntax is a crucial part of establishing an author's narrative voice. Ernest Hemingway, for example, is known for writing in very short, straightforward sentences, while James Joyce characteristically wrote in long, incredibly complicated lines.

- **Tone:** The mood or feeling of the text. Diction and syntax often contribute to the tone of a work. A novel written in short, clipped sentences that use small, simple words might feel brusque, cold, or matter-of-fact.

- **Imagery:** Language that appeals to the senses, representing things that can be seen, smelled, heard, tasted, or touched.

- **Figurative language:** Language that is not meant to be interpreted literally. The most common types of figurative language are *metaphors* and *similes,* which compare two unlike things in order to suggest a similarity between them—for example, "All the world's a stage," or "The moon is like a ball of green cheese." (Metaphors say one thing *is* another thing; similes claim that one thing is *like* another thing.)

---

3. CONSTRUCT A THESIS

When you've examined all the evidence you've collected and know how you want to answer the question, it's time to write your thesis statement. A *thesis* is a claim about a work of literature that needs to be supported by evidence and arguments. The thesis statement is the heart of the literary essay, and the bulk of your paper will be spent trying to prove this claim. A good thesis will be:

- **Arguable.** "*The Great Gatsby* describes New York society in the 1920s" isn't a thesis—it's a fact.

LITERARY ANALYSIS

- **Provable through textual evidence.** "*Hamlet* is a confusing but ultimately very well-written play" is a weak thesis because it offers the writer's personal opinion about the book. Yes, it's arguable, but it's not a claim that can be proved or supported with examples taken from the play itself.

- **Surprising.** "Both George and Lenny change a great deal in *Of Mice and Men*" is a weak thesis because it's obvious. A really strong thesis will argue for a reading of the text that is not immediately apparent.

- **Specific.** "Dr. Frankenstein's monster tells us a lot about the human condition" is *almost* a really great thesis statement, but it's still too vague. What does the writer mean by "a lot"? *How* does the monster tell us so much about the human condition?

GOOD THESIS STATEMENTS

Question: In *Romeo and Juliet*, which is more powerful in shaping the lovers' story: fate or foolishness?

Thesis: "Though Shakespeare defines Romeo and Juliet as 'star-crossed lovers' and images of stars and planets appear throughout the play, a closer examination of that celestial imagery reveals that the stars are merely witnesses to the characters' foolish activities and not the causes themselves."

Question: How does the bell jar function as a symbol in Sylvia Plath's *The Bell Jar*?

Thesis: "A bell jar is a bell-shaped glass that has three basic uses: to hold a specimen for observation, to contain gases, and to maintain a vacuum. The bell jar appears in each of these capacities in *The Bell Jar*, Plath's semi-autobiographical novel, and each appearances marks a different stage in Esther's mental breakdown."

Question: Would Piggy in *The Lord of the Flies* make a good island leader if he were given the chance?

Thesis: "Though the intelligent, rational, and innovative Piggy has the mental characteristics of a good leader, he ultimately lacks the social skills necessary to be an effective one. Golding emphasizes this point by giving Piggy a foil in the charismatic Jack, whose magnetic personality allows him to capture and wield power effectively, if not always wisely."

4. DEVELOP AND ORGANIZE ARGUMENTS

The reasons and examples that support your thesis will form the middle paragraphs of your essay. Since you can't really write your thesis statement until you know how you'll structure your argument, you'll probably end up working on steps 3 and 4 at the same time.

There's no single method of argumentation that will work in every context. One essay prompt might ask you to compare and contrast two characters, while another asks you to trace an image through a given work of literature. These questions require different kinds of answers and therefore different kinds of arguments. Below, we'll discuss three common kinds of essay prompts and some strategies for constructing a solid, well-argued case.

TYPES OF LITERARY ESSAYS

- **Compare and contrast**

  Compare and contrast the characters of Huck and Jim in THE ADVENTURES OF HUCKLEBERRY FINN.

  Chances are you've written this kind of essay before. In an academic literary context, you'll organize your arguments the same way you would in any other class. You can either go *subject by subject* or *point by point*. In the former, you'll discuss one character first and then the second. In the latter, you'll choose several traits (attitude toward life, social status, images and metaphors associated with the character) and devote a paragraph to each. You may want to use a mix of these two approaches—for example, you may want to spend a paragraph a piece broadly sketching Huck's and Jim's personalities before transitioning into a paragraph or two that describes a few key points of comparison. This can be a highly effective strategy if you want to make a counterintuitive argument—that, despite seeming to be totally different, the two objects being compared are actually similar in a very important way (or vice versa). Remember that your essay should reveal something fresh or unexpected about the text, so think beyond the obvious parallels and differences.

- **Trace**

  Choose an image—for example, birds, knives, or eyes—and trace that image throughout MACBETH.

  Sounds pretty easy, right? All you need to do is read the play, underline every appearance of a knife in *Macbeth,* and then list them in your essay in the order they appear, right? Well, not exactly. Your teacher doesn't want a simple catalog of examples. He or she wants to see you make *connections* between those examples—that's the difference between summarizing and analyzing. In the *Macbeth* example above, think about the different contexts in which knives appear in the play and to what effect. In *Macbeth*, there are real knives and imagined knives; knives that kill and knives that simply threaten. Categorize and classify your examples to give them some order. Finally, always keep the overall effect in mind. After you choose and analyze your examples, you should come to some greater understanding about the work, as well as your chosen image, symbol, or phrase's role in developing the major themes and stylistic strategies of that work.

- **Debate**

  Is the society depicted in 1984 good for its citizens?

  In this kind of essay, you're being asked to debate a moral, ethical, or aesthetic issue regarding the work. You might be asked to judge a character or group of characters (*Is Caesar responsible for his own demise?*) or the work itself (*Is JANE EYRE a feminist novel?*). For this kind of essay, there are two important points to keep in mind. First, don't simply base your arguments on your personal feelings and reactions. Every literary essay expects you to read and analyze the work, so search for evidence in the text. What do characters in *1984* have to say about the government of Oceania? What images does Orwell use that might give you a hint about his attitude toward the government? As in any debate, you also need to make sure that you define all the necessary terms before you begin to argue your case. What does it mean to be a "good" society? What makes a novel "feminist"? You should define your terms right up front, in the first paragraph after your introduction.

  Second, remember that strong literary essays make contrary and surprising arguments. Try to think outside the box. In the *1984* example above, it seems like the obvious answer would be no, the totalitarian society depicted in Orwell's novel is *not* good for its citizens. But can you think of any arguments for the opposite side? Even if your final assertion is that the novel depicts a cruel, repressive, and therefore harmful society, acknowledging and responding to the counterargument will strengthen your overall case.

5. WRITE THE INTRODUCTION

Your introduction sets up the entire essay. It's where you present your topic and articulate the particular issues and questions you'll be addressing. It's also where you, as the writer, introduce yourself to your readers. A persuasive literary essay immediately establishes its writer as a knowledgeable, authoritative figure.

An introduction can vary in length depending on the overall length of the essay, but in a traditional five-paragraph essay it should be no longer than one paragraph. However long it is, your introduction needs to:

- **Provide any necessary context.** Your introduction should situate the reader and let him or her know what to expect. What book are you discussing? Which characters? What topic will you be addressing?

- **Answer the "So what?" question.** Why is this topic important, and why is your particular position on the topic noteworthy? Ideally, your introduction should pique the reader's interest by suggesting how your argument is surprising or otherwise counterintuitive. Literary essays make unexpected connections and reveal less-than-obvious truths.

- **Present your thesis.** This usually happens at or very near the end of your introduction.

- **Indicate the shape of the essay to come.** Your reader should finish reading your introduction with a good sense of the scope of your essay as well as the path you'll take toward proving your thesis. You don't need to spell out every step, but you do need to suggest the organizational pattern you'll be using.

Your introduction should not:

- **Be vague.** Beware of the two killer words in literary analysis: *interesting* and *important*. Of course the work, question, or example is interesting and important—that's why you're writing about it!

- **Open with any grandiose assertions.** Many student readers think that beginning their essays with a flamboyant statement such as, "Since the dawn of time, writers have been fascinated with the topic of free will," makes them sound important and commanding. You know what? It actually sounds pretty amateurish.

- **Wildly praise the work.** Another typical mistake student writers make is extolling the work or author. Your teacher doesn't need to be told that "Shakespeare is perhaps the greatest writer in the English language." You can mention a work's reputation in passing—by referring to *The Adventures of Huckleberry Finn* as "Mark Twain's enduring classic," for example—but don't make a point of bringing it up unless that reputation is key to your argument.

- **Go off-topic.** Keep your introduction streamlined and to the point. Don't feel the need to throw in all kinds of bells and whistles in order to impress your reader—just get to the point as quickly as you can, without skimping on any of the required steps.

6. Write the Body Paragraphs

Once you've written your introduction, you'll take the arguments you developed in step 4 and turn them into your body paragraphs. The organization of this middle section of your essay will largely be determined by the argumentative strategy you use, but no matter how you arrange your thoughts, your body paragraphs need to do the following:

- **Begin with a strong topic sentence.** Topic sentences are like signs on a highway: they tell the reader where they are and where they're going. A good topic sentence not only alerts readers to what issue will be discussed in the following paragraph but also gives them a sense of what argument will be made *about* that issue. "Rumor and gossip play an important role in *The Crucible*" isn't a strong topic sentence because it doesn't tell us very much. "The community's constant gossiping creates an environment that allows false accusations to flourish" is a much stronger topic sentence—it not only tells us *what* the paragraph will discuss (gossip) but *how* the paragraph will discuss the topic (by showing how gossip creates a set of conditions that leads to the play's climactic action).

- **Fully and completely develop a single thought.** Don't skip around in your paragraph or try to stuff in too much material. Body paragraphs are like bricks: each individual

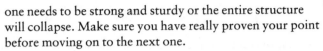

one needs to be strong and sturdy or the entire structure will collapse. Make sure you have really proven your point before moving on to the next one.

- **Use transitions effectively.** Good literary essay writers know that each paragraph must be clearly and strongly linked to the material around it. Think of each paragraph as a response to the one that precedes it. Use transition words and phrases such as *however, similarly, on the contrary, therefore,* and *furthermore* to indicate what kind of response you're making.

---

7. WRITE THE CONCLUSION

Just as you used the introduction to ground your readers in the topic before providing your thesis, you'll use the conclusion to quickly summarize the specifics learned thus far and then hint at the broader implications of your topic. A good conclusion will:

- **Do more than simply restate the thesis.** If your thesis argued that *The Catcher in the Rye* can be read as a Christian allegory, don't simply end your essay by saying, "And that is why *The Catcher in the Rye* can be read as a Christian allegory." If you've constructed your arguments well, this kind of statement will just be redundant.

- **Synthesize the arguments, not summarize them.** Similarly, don't repeat the details of your body paragraphs in your conclusion. The reader has already read your essay, and chances are it's not so long that they've forgotten all your points by now.

- **Revisit the "So what?" question.** In your introduction, you made a case for why your topic and position are important. You should close your essay with the same sort of gesture. What do your readers know now that they didn't know before? How will that knowledge help them better appreciate or understand the work overall?

- **Move from the specific to the general.** Your essay has most likely treated a very specific element of the work—a single character, a small set of images, or a particular passage. In your conclusion, try to show how this narrow discussion has wider implications for the work overall. If your essay on *To Kill a Mockingbird* focused on the character of Boo Radley, for example, you might want to include a bit in your conclusion about how he fits into the novel's larger message about childhood, innocence, or family life.

- **Stay relevant.** Your conclusion should suggest new directions of thought, but it shouldn't be treated as an opportunity to pad your essay with all the extra, interesting ideas you came up with during your brainstorming sessions but couldn't fit into the essay proper. Don't attempt to stuff in unrelated queries or too many abstract thoughts.

- **Avoid making overblown closing statements.** A conclusion should open up your highly specific, focused discussion, but it should do so without drawing a sweeping lesson about life or human nature. Making such observations may be part of the point of reading, but it's almost always a mistake in essays, where these observations tend to sound overly dramatic or simply silly.

A+ Essay Checklist

Congratulations! If you've followed all the steps we've outlined above, you should have a solid literary essay to show for all your efforts. What if you've got your sights set on an A+? To write the kind of superlative essay that will be rewarded with a perfect grade, keep the following rubric in mind. These are the qualities that teachers expect to see in a truly A+ essay. How does yours stack up?

- ✓ Demonstrates a thorough understanding of the book
- ✓ Presents an original, compelling argument
- ✓ Thoughtfully analyzes the text's formal elements
- ✓ Uses appropriate and insightful examples
- ✓ Structures ideas in a logical and progressive order
- ✓ Demonstrates a mastery of sentence construction, transitions, grammar, spelling, and word choice

SUGGESTED ESSAY TOPICS

1. *How does Faber define the value of books? Does his definition of "quality" apply to media other than printed books? Do you think his definitions are accurate or not? Explain.*

2. *Discuss Montag's relationship with Mildred. Is this a typical marital relationship in their culture? Discuss the role of family in the characters' lives, particularly in relation to the TV parlor "families" and their nature and function.*

3. *Discuss the use of quotations from literature in* FAHRENHEIT 451. *Which works are quoted and to what effect? Pay specific attention to "Dover Beach," the Bible, and quotes from Shakespeare.*

A+ Student Essay

What effect does Clarisse have on Montag?

Before Montag meets Clarisse, his sixteen-year-old neighbor, he is little more than an automaton, a book-burning robot. He reports to work, copes with his suicidal wife, and walks through his television-obsessed world, but he hardly notices what he is doing. Clarisse shakes Montag out of his stupor, forces him to examine the world around him, and inspires him to take drastic and violent steps. She does all of this indirectly, however. Her key function in the novel—the function that sets all of these changes in motion—is to show Montag what it means to be a writer.

Like a nascent novelist, Clarisse is keenly aware of and interested in the world she lives in. In a series of conversation, she shows Montag the way she observes society, savors lovely things, and reflects on what she sees. She shares her insights into people, expressing wonderment at the way they blather to each other without talking about anything meaningful, race past beautiful sights without observing them, and fail to educate children. She points out small details, such as the dew on the grass and the man in the moon. She delights in old superstitions, such as the idea that dandelions show whether someone is in love. She shares metaphors, comparing the rain to wine and the fallen leaves to cinnamon. She displays curiosity about other people's motivations and lives, asking Montag whether he is happy, and whether it's true that firefighters like him once put fires out rather than starting them. By speaking openly to Montag and showing him the way her mind works, she allows him to see the world through her eyes—the eyes of someone who actually thinks about what's going on around her and whose knack for observation makes her seem destined to become a writer.

Getting to know Clarisse inspires Montag to observe the world with the same writerly care she does. He turns from an automaton into a thinking, feeling, analyzing being. He looks at his deadened house and his emotionally stunted wife through new eyes. He starts wondering about the history of firefighting. He notices that most people care far more for their television families than they do for their real ones. He realizes that he is not in love with anyone, as Clarisse's lighthearted dandelion game indicated. Instead of drifting through society in an unthinking daze, without analyzing it, he begins to contemplate the way his countrymen live and how he fits into the social fabric. He begins to interrogate the ways in which he is similar to and different than his coworkers. He notices, for example, that all the other fireman look exactly as he does: dark-haired and unshaven, "mirror images" of Montag. At the same time, he realizes that his physical resemblance to the other firemen belies the hesitance he feels about performing his job, a hesitance the other firemen don't seem to share.

Once Montag understand what it means to think like a writer, he has a revelation about what it means to *be* a writer. He realizes that writers are people who think as Clarisse does (and as he is beginning to) and who then organize and shape their thoughts on paper. As he tells Mildred, it dawns on him that "'a man was behind each one of those books. A man had to think them up. A man had to take a long time to put them down on paper.'" For most of his adult life, he has thought of books simply as physical objects. Thanks to Clarisse, he understands that the books he is burning are products of human endeavor. They represent an individual writer's entire life, including his or her way of viewing the world. When he burns them, Montag realizes, he is symbolically burning writers like Clarisse. This revelation shows him how immoral his work is, and ultimately leads him to take brave and violent action.

Clarisse disappears fairly early on in the novel, but she is the key that unlocks Montag. She opens his eyes and inspires him to change. Although she is a bright, slightly naïve teenager, Clarisse is also the closest thing Bradbury has to a representative in the novel. With her eye for detail, her cutting social insight, and her passion for observation, she seems like the kind of girl who might go on to write a novel such as *Fahrenheit 451*.

GLOSSARY OF LITERARY TERMS

ANTAGONIST

The entity that acts to frustrate the goals of the *protagonist*. The antagonist is usually another *character* but may also be a non-human force.

ANTIHERO / ANTIHEROINE

A *protagonist* who is not admirable or who challenges notions of what should be considered admirable.

CHARACTER

A person, animal, or any other thing with a personality that appears in a *narrative*.

CLIMAX

The moment of greatest intensity in a text or the major turning point in the *plot*.

CONFLICT

The central struggle that moves the *plot* forward. The conflict can be the *protagonist*'s struggle against fate, nature, society, or another person.

FIRST-PERSON POINT OF VIEW

A literary style in which the *narrator* tells the story from his or her own *point of view* and refers to himself or herself as "I." The narrator may be an active participant in the story or just an observer.

HERO / HEROINE

The principal *character* in a literary work or *narrative*.

IMAGERY

Language that brings to mind sense-impressions, representing things that can be seen, smelled, heard, tasted, or touched.

MOTIF

A recurring idea, structure, contrast, or device that develops or informs the major *themes* of a work of literature.

NARRATIVE

A story.

NARRATOR

The person (sometimes a *character*) who tells a story; the *voice* assumed by the writer. The narrator and the author of the work of literature are not the same person.

PLOT

The arrangement of the events in a story, including the sequence in which they are told, the relative emphasis they are given, and the causal connections between events.

POINT OF VIEW

The *perspective* that a *narrative* takes toward the events it describes.

PROTAGONIST

The main *character* around whom the story revolves.

SETTING

The location of a *narrative* in time and space. Setting creates mood or atmosphere.

SUBPLOT

A secondary *plot* that is of less importance to the overall story but may serve as a point of contrast or comparison to the main plot.

SYMBOL

An object, *character,* figure, or color that is used to represent an abstract idea or concept. Unlike an *emblem,* a symbol may have different meanings in different contexts.

SYNTAX

The way the words in a piece of writing are put together to form lines, phrases, or clauses; the basic structure of a piece of writing.

THEME

A fundamental and universal idea explored in a literary work.

TONE

The author's attitude toward the subject or *characters* of a story or poem or toward the reader.

VOICE

An author's individual way of using language to reflect his or her own personality and attitudes. An author communicates voice through *tone, diction,* and *syntax.*

A Note on Plagiarism

Plagiarism—presenting someone else's work as your own—rears its ugly head in many forms. Many students know that copying text without citing it is unacceptable. But some don't realize that even if you're not quoting directly, but instead are paraphrasing or summarizing, *it is plagiarism* unless you cite the source.

Here are the most common forms of plagiarism:

- Using an author's phrases, sentences, or paragraphs without citing the source
- Paraphrasing an author's ideas without citing the source
- Passing off another student's work as your own

How do you steer clear of plagiarism? You should *always* acknowledge all words and ideas that aren't your own by using quotation marks around verbatim text or citations like footnotes and endnotes to note another writer's ideas. For more information on how to give credit when credit is due, ask your teacher for guidance or visit www.sparknotes.com.

REVIEW & RESOURCES

QUIZ

1. What is the significance of the title *Fahrenheit 451*?

   A. It is the maximum temperature of most ovens.
   B. It is the temperature at which germanium melts.
   C. It is the temperature at which paper ignites and burns.
   D. It is the temperature at which an Easy-Bake oven self-destructs.

2. According to mythology, what is the salamander's relation to fire?

   A. It lives in it.
   B. It eats it.
   C. It hates it.
   D. It is delicious roasted in it.

3. How many times can the phoenix be reborn from its ashes?

   A. One
   B. Three
   C. Nine
   D. An unlimited number

4. Which of Clarisse's relatives influenced her the most?

   A. Her mother
   B. Her father
   C. Her uncle
   D. Her grandfather

5. What was the occupation of Granger's grandfather?

   A. Fireman
   B. Sculptor
   C. Racecar driver
   D. Senator

6. Which of the following Shakespeare tragedies does Beatty quote immediately before his death?

    A. *Hamlet*
    B. *Macbeth*
    C. *Othello*
    D. *Julius Caesar*

7. Which of the following books of the Bible does Faber read to Montag over the radio?

    A. Ecclesiastes
    B. The Book of Job
    C. Revelations
    D. Deuteronomy

8. What are the earplug radios in the novel called?

    A. Seashells
    B. Whistlers
    C. Flutes
    D. White Clowns

9. What animal metaphor does Montag use to describe the stomach pump and blood-replacement machine used on Mildred?

    A. Hound
    B. Fish
    C. Salamander
    D. Snake

10. Which woman cries when Montag reads poetry?

    A. Mildred
    B. Clarisse
    C. Mrs. Phelps
    D. Mrs. Bowles

11. What is Clarisse's last name?

    A.   McClellan
    B.   Faber
    C.   Phelps
    D.   Granger

12. How does Mildred claim Clarisse is killed?

    A.   In a fire
    B.   By a car
    C.   By a drug overdose
    D.   By the Hound

13. How many legs does the Hound have?

    A.   Eight
    B.   Six
    C.   Four
    D.   Three

14. Which drug does the Hound inject into Montag?

    A.   Codeine
    B.   Procaine
    C.   Morphine
    D.   Psilocybin

15. What is the name of the toothpaste advertised on the subway?

    A.   Crain's Crest
    B.   Finchman's Fluoride Wonder
    C.   Abel's AquaFresh
    D.   Denham's Dentifrice

16. In whose home does Montag plant books?

    A.   Black's
    B.   Stoneman's
    C.   Beatty's
    D.   McClellan's

17. What position did Faber hold before he retired?

    A. Printer
    B. Librarian
    C. Professor of history
    D. Professor of English

18. Which poem does Montag read to Mildred and her friends?

    A. "The Lovesong of J. Alfred Prufrock"
    B. "Ode on a Grecian Urn"
    C. "Dover Beach"
    D. "The Flea"

19. What colors are the firemen's uniforms?

    A. Blue and red
    B. Black and orange
    C. Yellow and gray
    D. Orange and red

20. What kind of liquor does Faber give Montag before he flees to the country?

    A. Whiskey
    B. Vodka
    C. Rum
    D. Gin

21. How long a time period does the novel cover?

    A. About two months
    B. About a year
    C. Three days
    D. A little over three weeks

22. What does Granger's group do before heading for the city after the bombing?

    A. Eat breakfast
    B. Pray
    C. Burn their books
    D. Hold hands

23. What does Montag follow to reach the Book People in the country?

   A. The river and the railroad tracks
   B. The river and the highway
   C. The river and the cowpath
   D. The artery tunnel and the highway

24. What happens to the old woman whose house is burned by the firemen?

   A. She refuses to leave and dies in the fire.
   B. She is taken to a mental institution.
   C. She is put in jail.
   D. She disappears mysteriously.

25. In what city did Montag meet Mildred?

   A. The unspecified city in which the novel is set
   B. New York
   C. Philadelphia
   D. Chicago

SUGGESTIONS FOR FURTHER READING

BLOOM, HAROLD, ed. *Ray Bradbury's* FAHRENHEIT 451: *Bloom's Modern Critical Interpretations*. New York: Chelsea House Publishing, 2001.

———. *Ray Bradbury: Modern Critical Views*. New York: Chelsea House Publishing, 2001.

BRADBURY, RAY. *Bradbury Stories: 100 of His Most Celebrated Tales*. New York: Harper Perennial, 2005.

———. *Dandelion Wine*. New York: Avon Books, 1999.

———. FAHRENHEIT 451 *and Related Readings*. New York: McDougal Littell & Co., 1997.

———. *The Martian Chronicles*. New York: Bantam Books, 1994.

———. *Zen in the Art of Writing: Essays on Creativity (Expanded)*. Santa Barbara, CA: Joshua Odell Editions, 1994.

DE KOSTER, KATIE, ed. *Readings on* FAHRENHEIT 451: *Greenhaven Press Literary Companion to American Literature*. New York: Greenhaven Press, 2000.

REID, ROBIN ANNE. *Ray Bradbury: A Critical Companion*. Westport, CT: Greenwood Press, 2000.

WELLER, SAM. *The Bradbury Chronicles: The Life of Ray Bradbury*. New York: William Morrow, 2005.